Best Staffordshire Walks

Les Lumsdon

First Edition *(published as 'Staffordshire Walks, Simply Superb')*
Copyright © L.M. Lumsdon, 1988
Reprinted 1988, 1990, 1991

This Revised Edition:
Copyright © L.M. Lumsdon, 1996

Published by Sigma Leisure – an imprint of
Sigma Press, 1 South Oak Lane, Wilmslow, Cheshire SK9 6AR, England.

British Library Cataloguing in Publication Data
A CIP record for this book is available from the British Library.

ISBN: 1-85058-564-4

Typesetting and Design by: Sigma Press, Wilmslow, Cheshire.

Cover photograph: 'Walking on the Roaches' (Staffordshire County Council)

Maps: Pam Upchurch

Illustrations: Transport Marketing Ltd, Birmingham

Printed by: MFP Design and Print

Disclaimer: the information in this book is given in good faith and is believed to be correct at the time of publication. No responsibility is accepted by either the author or publisher for errors or omissions, or for any loss or injury howsoever caused. Only you can judge your own fitness, competence and experience.

Contents

STAFFORDSHIRE VILLAGES 97

THE WALKS

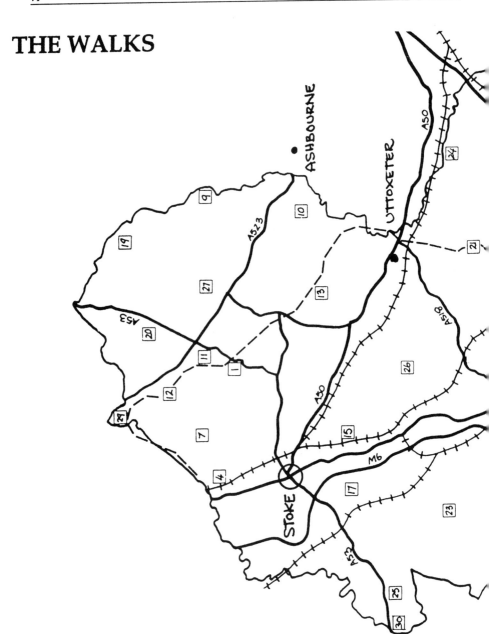

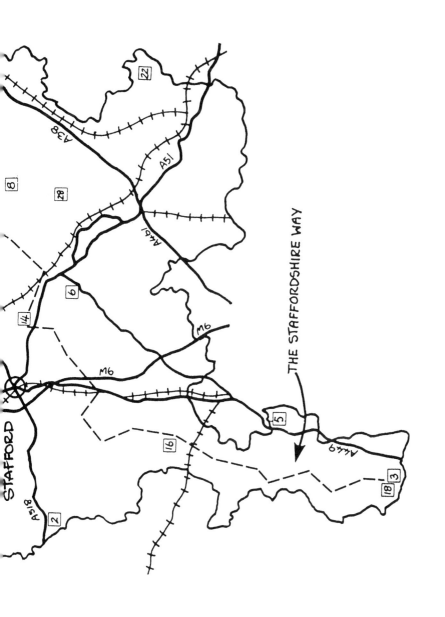

The Conservatory, Weston Park (walk 16)

Introduction

Staffordshire's remarkable county

From around the globe, travellers make their way to visit the home of English china, to spend a day at one of Europe's foremost leisure parks, Alton Towers, or to follow in the footsteps of one of Staffordshire's famous sons or daughters, but few travel beyond recognised routes to taste the richness and variety of Staffordshire's beautiful countryside. The county is largely undiscovered. Even walkers tend not to venture much beyond Cannock Chase, that most famous of the ancient Midland forests, or deviate from favourite places in the Staffordshire Moorlands. Yet, within five miles of any Staffordshire town, superb walking country, forgotten lanes and tracks, and little-used footpaths lead to and from enchanting villages not much touched by the passing years.

Varied Scenery

What makes Staffordshire so attractive to the walker? The answer is simple – the variety of scenery that can be viewed within such short distances. For example, from Shugborough Hall you can walk along level canal towpaths through the sweeping floodplains of the Trent to landscaped gardens of character, to monuments of considerable historic interest, to Christopher Wren's Chapel at Ingestre or the fine Elizabethan gatehouse at Tixall. Equally, within a mile or so you can be climbing up wooded banks from Milford Common into Cannock Chase, less than 20 minutes from Shugborough and a very contrasting landscape.

From Moors to Parkland

It is the same the county over. There are walks in parkland, through gently rolling farming country, along edges and woodland, by the swirling pools of Staffordshire's rivers and all within close proximity of each other. The very north of the county differs, however. It is a paradise for those who like the wide expanses, the dramatic moorland scenery, the drystone walls and limestone valleys. The Staffordshire

Moorlands belong to the Pennines and as such includes part of the Peak District National Park.

Unusual Attractions

Staffordshire countryside is also appealing because there are so many attractions situated in distinctly rural settings. The canals and country houses, restored mills and steam railway centres, glass-making and craft workshops are features of the landscape. This is the world of the discriminating traveller. These are the places we love to call into, to spend an hour or two delving into history or watching a skilful craftsperson create an artefact to delight. You will find that most of the walks either feature an attraction of some description or are situated within a short distance from one. This makes for a really good day out: perhaps enjoying a walk, taking lunch at a wayside pub or cafe, then an hour or two at a local attraction before journeying home.

The Staffordshire Way

A number of the walks included use or are situated near to parts of the Staffordshire Way. This long distance footpath, created by Staffordshire County Council, stretches 92 miles between Mow Cop and Kinver Edge. In 1995 several Ramblers' groups in association with the County Council undertook a survey and programme of restoration work to improve waymarking, stiles, bridges and the like. The Ramblers have also published an accommodation leaflet for the Way. Sigma publish a guide to the Staffordshire Way by Lumsdon and Rushton which is available from Tourist Information Centres and local bookshops. This includes a number of circular walks from the Staffordshire Way as well as a description of the route itself.

In recent years the County Council and district authorities have set about improving the footpath network. Staffordshire Moorlands District Council, for example, produces a number of leaflets outlining circular walks in the Moorlands. There's also a series of booklets published by Newcastle Borough in association with a keen local rambler, which are available locally. Lichfield and Stafford produce similar which are sold locally. There are also dozens of examples of such local enterprise, like Kinder where the Civic Society has published leaflets illustrating local walks. This can only add to the retention of our footpath heritage and to the enjoyment of the countryside by those of us who seek the quiet bye-ways. Much of the network is slowly but surely being re opened but some landowners still pay scant regard to the law by ploughing up paths, obstructing the way with barbed wire and other impediments which make the going difficult on occasion. Opinion is very much against them.

Easy Travel

One point that is very often overlooked by the walker is the accessibility of Staffordshire from Greater Manchester and the West Midlands. Within not much more than an hour, you can be out walking a footpath in the area of your choice. Several of the walks are served by bus and train, so the trip can still be made by public transport. It can so much enhance the journey when you're not in a rush. The bus and train enable you to look at the countryside at leisure, to peer over hedges and walls, as well as meeting people travelling between town and village going about their daily business. The author firmly supports the Countrygoer campaign which seeks to encourage people to use public transport to get into the countryside wherever possible.

Basic public transport details are included at the beginning of each walk, but for up-to-date information 'phone STAFFORDSHIRE BUSLINE on Cannock (01543) 577099 Stafford (01785) 223344, or Stoke-on-Trent (01782) 206608.

The Walks

The walks range from very easy going to those in slightly more difficult terrain. They vary in distance from three to ten miles and are walkable in all seasons. The essential information you need to read before setting out on one is included at the beginning of each walk. In this way, for example, a family will be able to choose an easily paced walk stopping off, possibly, at a local cafe or a suitable picnic place before returning. On the other hand, someone looking for a longer walk in rougher terrain, which requires more effort, will find these marked up as well. The choice is yours.

The suggested walking times are merely for guidance. If you like a vigorously paced walk, then these will be generous; but if you like to savour the countryside they'll not be far wrong. All of the walks involve climbing over stiles of varying descriptions. The term 'stile', could describe anything from a set of steps over a drystone wall to a jumble of wood lying between two bushes. Directions are given assuming your back is to the stile every time you cross a field boundary. The walks should be easy to follow using the route descriptions and the maps, although not detailed, provide further guidance.

For many people, the use of maps is fun. By all means, use the Ordnance Survey 1:50,000 scale Landranger Maps which are adequate, but the best for walking are the green-covered Pathfinder series 1:25,000 or the larger yellow Outdoor Leisure Map 'The White Peak' which is especially useful for walks in the Staffordshire Moorlands. Cannock Chase is covered by the newer Ordnance Survey Explorer map 6. Understanding the features of the landscape and what has happened in the past improves the enjoyment of the walk considerably. Maps help in this process. Studying those little plots on the landscape, the shape of the field boundaries marked up on the Pathfinder maps, the look of settlements, the routes of ancient tracks no longer trodden by pack horses or rutted by wagons, all add to an understanding of the countryside and help to unfold its hidden secrets.

If you do not like using maps, however, do not worry. The walks are easily achievable using the guidance notes in each chapter. Many of the walks are fairly straightforward, following clearly definable paths and tracks. Others require a little more detective work!

All of the walks have been researched on the ground but there will always be changes to the environment. Trees and bushes may be cleared, arable crops sown where grassland lay before. No better example can be found than on the Loggerheads to Burnt Wood walk where several acres of woodland have been felled and grass sown once again, something that is not easily recognisable from the map. Land use changes over time. I can only apologise for such things in advance but common-sense will prevail when on the route.

One matter which sometimes causes concern is what to do when you cross a stile and before you is a crop and no reinstated footpath. Rights of way are literally what they mean. You are entitled to walk without obstruction along the way to your chosen destination. Sometimes, especially if you have young ones with you, this becomes an impracticability and the nearest diversion becomes the order of the day, possibly skirting around a field edge. The same applies to woodland sections. Fallen trees which have not been cleared by the owner for some time tend to lead to straight paths becoming rather more winding than expected. The path in Gold's Wood above Ellastone fits this description well. Any serious obstructions, however, should be reported to the Highways Authority, which, in this case, is Staffordshire County Council. Only in this way will we maintain a network of paths open for the enjoyment of others.

We sometimes tend to forget, however, that this is a working countryside. For example, some of the tracks are used by farmers to lead their cows in for milking, others pass through naturally wet areas. Be prepared for mud on some of the walks! It is essential to wear the right footwear. In drier months it might be possible to use heavy shoes or even trainers, but after rain and in the winter months when water is lying on the ground, boots or wellingtons are strongly advised.

Rambling near Alton

On a few of the walks in areas such as Cannock Chase, the Hanchurch Hills, or near the Harecastle Tunnels, some of the paths are made of a harder, compact surface and are fairly well-drained throughout the year. The others are not. Be prepared for the wetter ones.

It is equally wise to always carry rainwear. On these walks you do not need to be prepared for the Himalayas, but take outdoor clothing that is really waterproof and a spare woolly in case the weather turns. You can often manage these items, along with a snack and the basics of a first aid kit, in a small knapsack without discomfort.

Please treat the life and work of the countryside with respect. Keep, wherever possible, to the footpaths and take all litter home. The golden rules are summed up in the Country Code.

Above all else, enjoy yourself in some of Staffordshire's loveliest countryside ... it is a rather underestimated county for walking.

Staffordshire's Canal Heritage

The Canal Era was as much of a shock to rural residents in 18th century England as motorways are to country lovers today. Not since the Romans had the populace witnessed such major feats of engineering. Not only did the building of the canals draw to quiet locations hundreds of burly navvies it also brought the construction of major earthworks, canalside buildings, locks and tunnels which considerably altered the landscape. The scale of the structures and the distinctive architecture, however, seem to have blended well into the rural surroundings, something that would be difficult to say about our 20th century highways.

Extensive Network

The surviving canal system in Staffordshire is extensive, perhaps amounting to the greatest mileage in any of the shire counties. There are a number of reasons for this. One reason is the desire of early industrialists in the Potteries to be able to transport raw materials more cheaply and at the same time provide reliable channels for their finished goods. One of the major initiators of the Trent and Mersey canal in the 1760s was Josiah Wedgwood. He was looking for a way to obtain a regular flow of china clay through the port of Liverpool to Etruria and at an acceptable price. Hence, his sustained commitment to the Trent and Mersey project. Another key reason is that these early entrepreneurs looked to ways of creating navigations across the entire width of the country from Hull to Liverpool, and also to link up the West Coast with the Midlands and beyond. While their interest was of a local nature, they also looked eagerly to the provision of a wider workable network. It is a tribute to such industrialists that so much was built and in such a sturdy fashion. The projects often took far longer than predicted and required far more capital than at first anticipated, often with the prospect of little return in the short-term.

A Tribute to the Navvies

The network that survives so well in the county is also a tribute to the thousands of tradesmen and navvies who worked under the greatest canal engineers of the time, masters such as James Brindley and Thomas Telford. The work involved long hours of sweat in appalling conditions. The key canals, some with smaller branches, are still intact today for us to use for recreational purposes. They include the Caldon Branch from Etruria to Froghall, the Shropshire Union coming into the county near Market Drayton and following a course along the Shropshire Border to Autherley Junction north of Wolverhampton, the Staffordshire and Worcestershire canal parting company with the Trent and Mersey at Great Haywood and running down to Kinver and on to Stourport by the Severn. Finally, there's the Trent and Mersey coming in near to Kidsgrove, making its way through the heart of the industrial Potteries, then onwards to Burton-upon-Trent.

The four walks outlined below allow you to explore the towpaths of these canals. They provide only a sample of the potential mileage that could be walked along Staffordshire's canals. Most sections are in good enough order to walk with ease, but care has to be taken in some places where the path narrows or the banks are eroded. The towpaths are not always rights of ways but British Waterways welcomes walkers who take pleasure in discovering canals. They do, after all, offer tranquil passageways through otherwise busy areas. That's one of their most noticeable features. They were built to fuel industrial development, yet have remained so rural and undeveloped for most of their lengths.

The structures remain, but the canal culture has all but vanished. As most canals lost commercial traffic in the early part of this century, so a way of life has been lost. It must have been a very hard existence for the boatmen, sometimes with family on board, working long hours to meet relentless deadlines. If you have been on board a powered narrowboat, you'll know how difficult it is to make headway against a biting wind and ruffled water. Imagine the difficulty with a horse drawn vessel. It had its freedoms, nevertheless, and compensations such as the canalside drinking houses. Some of these old houses survive such as the likes of The Anchor at Grub Street near Woodseaves or the Black Lion at Consall Forge on the Caldon. They serve a different clientele now, but the relics on the bar walls help to conjure up an image of the boatpeople in those early days.

WALK 1: Cheddleton to Denford, and the Caldon Canal

A walk through traditional upland farming to Cats Edge, then into the Churnet Valley by way of the Caldon Canal towpath. One or two climbs but mainly a gentle walk predominantly across fields and along the towpath.

Distance: 6 miles (9.5km)

Time: Allow 3 hours

Map: Pathfinder Sheet SJ 85/95 Leek and Kidsgrove.

How To Get There:

By Car – Cheddleton is on the main A520 road between Stoke-on-Trent and Leek. There are two lay-by sections at the top of the village suitable for parking.

By Bus – There is an hourly service Hanley to Leek, including Sundays, and an hourly service Mondays to Saturdays between Longton and Leek.

Refreshments and Accommodation: There are several public houses in Cheddleton. You pass by the Black Lion by the church in Cheddleton and also the Hollybush at Denford *en route*. Bed and breakfast is available in the Cheddleton area.

Nearest Tourist Information: Leek, Telephone (01538) 381000.

The walk begins in Cheddleton. If travelling by bus it is easy enough to begin at the Flint Mill. If you are travelling by car it is more difficult to park in the village so try the lay-by at the top end of the village on the main A520 road. Go right down Ostlers Lane towards Cheddleton church, (dedicated to St Edward the Confessor and dating partly from the 12th century). Nearby is the Black Lion pub and ancient village stocks for those inclined to naughtiness! At the junction, however, you turn left into Shaffalong Lane by the new school. Beyond the old

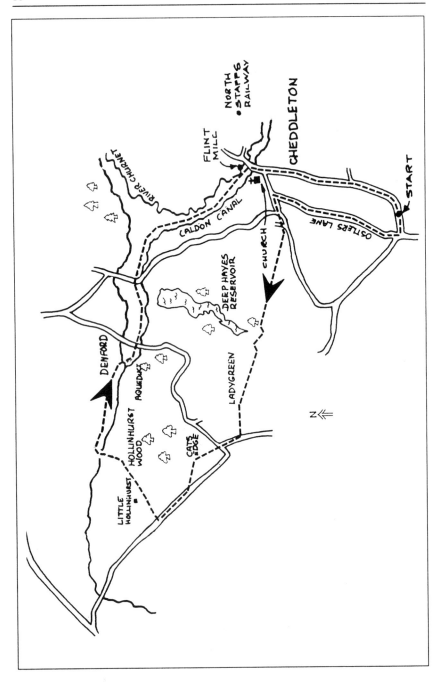

school, now a craft centre, there's a gap stile ahead with the path signed to Cats Edge.

To Cats Edge

Follow the path (which is waymarked as a Deep Hayes County Park circular ramble) to the next two stiles which guard a track leading to Hanfield Farm on the right. Proceed slightly right up the field to a stone and wooden stile which you cross. Head slightly right towards stiles situated at the far end of the line of trees, cross them and continue ahead for 50 metres, where upon you'll find the next stile on your right. From here aim for the electricity transmission poles with a line of trees in the background. Cross a stile and head in a similar direction. Cross the stile by a barred gate and follow the L-shaped track around to another stile and gate. In the next field, bear slightly left across to a stile which can just be seen beyond a small mound.

The path descends through the bushes. It falls steeply at first then curves right to skirt wet ground to another stile by two gateposts. Cross the stile and drop steeply down to a stream. Several paths are sign-posted here at the border of Deep Hayes Country Park.

If you would like to shorten the walk, bear right once over the footbridge and follow the waymarked route to the car-park and visitor centre within the park. You walk down the entrance road to Park Lane, turn left and then once over the bridge go right on to the Caldon Canal for Cheddleton.

Otherwise, follow the path ahead up a muddy section almost beneath a holly bush, then bear right up the bank to a stile leading into a meadow. The path follows the field's edge ahead, then left along a tractor track to the top left-hand corner where you join a road by Lee House. Turn right.

Walk to the junction and go through a gap stile by a barred gate. Continue ahead to the two stiles guarding the sleeper footbridge and make your way down the slope to the track. Follow this ahead and upwards towards Ladygreen Farm. Before reaching the farm buildings bear left up the perimeter hedge. The path runs through nettles and over old walling. Go over a stile into a field. Turn right to proceed up the bank to the road, where you turn right for the short distance to the T-junction known as Cats Edge.

This windswept spot offers good views of the surrounding area. It is hard to imagine that you are but a few miles away from the Potteries conurbation. At the road junction, go over the stile by the barred gate and keep ahead to the next gateway. There's a farmhouse to your left down the field. Go over a stile at another gateway and your way is still ahead with the wall to your left. Look out for the second field boundary on your left. There's a stone stile on your left at this point but it is not easy to recognise. Cross it and your way is ahead with the wall on your left, to the next field boundary by a trough. Continue ahead to a stile by a barred gate with a cottage on the left. Join the road, bear left, and then turn right onto a busier road which descends the hill.

It is a short walk to the entrance drive to Little Hollinhurst. Hayes Farm on the right. Go right into it then immediately right over a stile into the field. Then bear slightly left through the field keeping 30 metres to the right of the bungalow and buildings. You will see the stile in the first boundary. Cross it and aim in a similar direction in the next pasture. Cross a stile in a holly hedge and bear slightly left across the field to cross another stile Now, head slightly right towards a stile beneath an oak tree and you will see Hollinhurst Farm beyond. Once over the stile go slightly left towards the end of the long barn wall.

Cross a stile by the gate and walk to the metalled barred gate in the next boundary. Once over, you can see the canal and lock keeper's house. Aim for it.

The Caldon Canal

Built in the late 1760s and eventually reaching Froghall in 1776, the Caldon was built to transport coal, iron ore and limestone. Thanks to a number of interested parties, in particular the Caldon Canal Society, this navigation is open from its junction with the Trent and Mersey at Etruria to Froghall Wharf. From here onwards it is a very beautiful passage.

The path runs over a bridge at Hazelhurst Locks. You cut left by a building to join the towpath. On approaching the locks, the beautiful iron towpath bridge to the left, dating from 1842, strikes the walker immediately. Many of the fine stone bridges on this section are impressive too. They are the work of John Rennie, the engineer responsible for the canal's design features following Brindley's death. In fact, Brindley was out surveying at the canal's terminus and, unfortunately, caught a very bad chill. Biographers cite this as the key factor in the final stage of his failing health. The esteemed physician and scholar Erasmus Darwin attended to him but with no lasting curative. Within a matter of days he died.

Hazelhurst Locks, Caldon Canal

Hazelhurst Aqueduct

You go left down the flight of locks. It seems unusual, as logic tells you to turn right for the Churnet Valley! Not so. The other canal forms the Leek arm of the Caldon and is equally pleasant. The reason for the direction is soon unfolded. You walk under the Hazelhurst Aqueduct, dating from 1841 and continue to Denford as the Leek branch swings away above you. Pass by the Hollybush pub, then also at the next bridge, the entrance to Deep Hayes Park. From here onwards, it is a very pleasant stretch with the River Churnet nearby, as you progress to Cheddleton. The Flint Mill soon appears as the canal curves into the village.

Cheddleton's Attractions

Cheddleton Flint Mill houses two restored working water-wheels of different sizes, once used to grind flints for use in pottery making. The flint used to be despatched by boat to The Potteries along the Caldon Canal. The mill worked commercially up until 1963 and in 1967 the Cheddleton Flint Mill Industrial Heritage Trust began to restore the mill as a museum. It is now open to the public at weekends, but please check times with the Tourist Information Centre in Leek if travelling particularly to visit the mill. Not much further along the canal is access to the headquarters of the North Staffordshire Railway Company, situated at Cheddleton Railway Station. It is said to have been designed by the famous architect of the last century, Pugin, and many of the stations on the Churnet Valley Line were as impressive as Cheddleton. The railway centre is generally open throughout the summer months and on Sundays there is often an engine in steam, but please check opening times before setting out. The mission of the company is to operate a steam railway through the Churnet Valley to Froghall and possibly Oakamoor.

A few paces from the Flint Mill and you're back on the main road into Cheddleton Village.

WALK 2: The 'Shroppie' – Norbury Junction to Shelmore

Easy walking through a gentle landscape and along the towpath of the Shropshire Union Canal. Very short distance of road walking.

Distance: 2 miles (4km)

Time: Allow 1 hour

Map: Pathfinder Sheet SJ 62/72 Hodnet and Norbury and Sheet SJ 82/92 Stafford.

How To Get There:

By Car – A519 road between Eccleshall and Newport. Take turnings for Norbury and Norbury Junction. There is limited car parking near to the canal basin.

By Bus – A few journeys per week to Norbury village.

Refreshments and Accommodation: Soft drinks and food available at the canalside shop. The Junction Inn stands right next to the canal. Limited amount of bed and breakfast accommodation is available in the area, but there's more at Eccleshall and Newport, both being very attractive settlements.

Nearest Tourist Information: Stafford (01785) 40204

This walk starts at the entrance to the boatyard and canalside. Bear right down the road, which is very quiet, except on Sunday afternoons. As it bends sharply towards the canal embankment and by the entrance to a fishery, continue straight ahead on the bridle-path which runs along the edge of a wood on your right. There is about a mile stretch with a number of boundary fences to cross. Simply continue ahead.

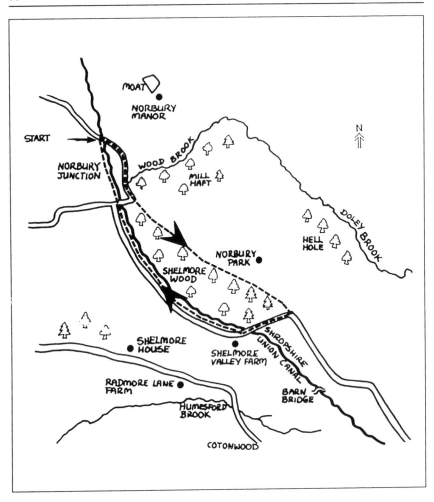

Lord Anson's Pheasants

Norbury Park is on your left and you'll see quite a few pheasants about in the fields and hedges. Thereby hangs a tale, for if it were not for Lord Anson's desire to protect his estate for pheasant shooting the line of the Shropshire Union Canal would have been somewhat different and far easier in engineering terms. You'll see the difference this diversion made on the return leg of the walk. Having maintained a way ahead for several fields, you come to an access drive from a farm which comes in from the left and which passes by Shelmore lodge.

At the road bear right for the short distance to the canal. Take care on this stretch, particularly the walk through the tunnel to the other side of the canal. Climb up the steps on your left to the towpath and turn left.

Shelmore Great Bank

This massive embankment, known as Shelmore Great Bank, caused the backers of the canal financial heartbreak and nearly toppled the engineer, Thomas Telford, from his position as engineering supremo of the project – all for the sake of Lord Anson's pheasants! The 66 mile line between Ellesmere Port and Autherley near Wolverhampton had not been an easy route throughout but this section confounded the engineers of the time. Can you imagine what the scene would have been like in 1832 when over 400 men and 70 horses were gathered to build up the embankment? There was collapse after collapse and it was only made sound in 1835, a year after Telford's death. The scale of the project can only be appreciated when you are overlooking the surrounding countryside from the towpath above.

The Last Great Narrowboat Canal

It was in the 1840s that the canal was taken over by a railway company, which became the Shropshire Union Railways and Canal Company. Fortunately, the idea of laying a railway track along the canal route did not come to fruition and until the First World War the canal functioned very successfully, unlike most of its counterparts elsewhere. This was the last great narrowboat canal to be built in England, at a time when railways were starting to gain in ascendancy. In some respects, its prosperity reflected not only the lack of railway development *en route* but also the steady management of the navigation.

The return section is easy enough, a mile or so along the towpath to Norbury Junction. Speaking of which you pass over a bridge which crosses the branch to Newport and East Shropshire, of which only a short distance remains in water. Looking at Norbury Junction, very much a self-contained community created by the Canal Era, and the stretches leading off in either direction, one begins to realise what a very rural canal the Shropshire Union is. It will, no doubt, have an increasing leisure role to play in the next century.

WALK 3: The Staffordshire and Worcestershire Canal

Kinver to Gibbet Wood returning via Whittington. Mainly gentle climbs across farmland with a lovely last section along the Staffordshire and Worcestershire Canal.

Distance: 4 miles (7.5km)

Time: Allow: 2 hours

Map: Pathfinder Sheet SO 88/98 Stourbridge.

How To Get There:

By Car – Travel on the A449 to Stourton and, just beyond the Stewponey Inn turn right into Dunsley Road for Kinver. There are a number of carparks in Kinver.

By Bus – There is a regular train service Mondays to Saturdays to Stourbridge. The West Midlands Travel bus runs hourly from here to Kinver.

Refreshments and Accommodation: Kinver has a number of cafes, restaurants and inns. Bed and breakfast accommodation is available.

Nearest Tourist Information: Travellers Joy on the High Street, Tel: (01384) 872940

Start at The White Hart public house on the High Street. Turn right and follow the main road to the river and canal. As the High Street curves to the left, a pleasant diversion is to pass by the Cross pub and the half timbered old Grammar School House, turning left down a narrow thoroughfare to Dunsley Road again. The Grammar School House, now a private dwelling, dates from the early 16th century and has been beautifully restored. Continue to the canal bridge.

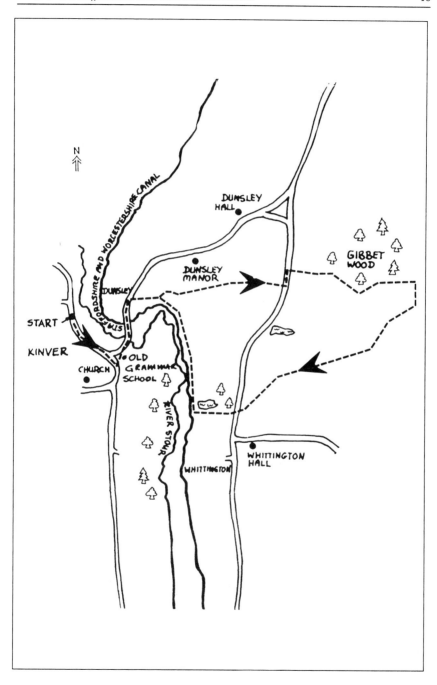

The Canal

This is the first sight of the Staffordshire and Worcestershire Canal and you often see boats negotiating the lock here. Built in the late 1760s and opened for traffic in 1772, this canal, financed by a prominent Wolverhampton businessman, brought a fair amount of trade to Kinver itself as well as substantial through traffic. It is still fairly busy with pleasure boats, especially during the school holidays. Not many miles away the Stourbridge canal joins it near Stourton but the Staffordshire and Worcestershire is prettier by far.

The Vine pub stands on your left and, shortly on your right, just beyond the bus stop and post box is a quiet lane, named 'Gibraltar', leading off right. The track continues down towards the canal. You, however, need to take the path which runs upwards through a wood until you reach a junction. Dunsley Hall, a fine looking building is on your right. The path continues ahead circling the perimeter of Dunsley. You come to a stile. Cross it and continue ahead to a stile mid-field with Dunsley Manor to your left in the foreground. There's a good view of the gentle landscape bordering Stourbridge from here.

Continue ahead once again to the main A449 road. The path descends slightly and the stiles act as markers for direction. The two latter fields very often have arable crops growing, but the right of way through these fields runs directly between clearly defined stiles.

Gibbet Wood

Cross the road and bear left along the wide verge. It is a very short stretch before the next gate on the right. Go over the stile next to it and keep company with the hedge on your left as the path rises up to the Gibbet Wood. This name evidently dates from 1813 when a William Howe was found guilty by Stafford Assizes of murdering Mr Benjamin Robins of Dunsley Hall. Sentences were harsh in those days and Howe's body was hung in chains in this vicinity.

At the next stile, turn left. This leads to an unsurfaced lane. Turn right and walk towards Roundhill Sewerage Farm. Fortunately, before reaching it there is a stile on your right. Cross over it and, keeping the hedge to your right, cross over another stile leading in to a rough patch. Go over the next stile and bear right down a path between the hedge and a line of trees. This section can get overgrown at times, so be prepared to trample the vegetation. Cross over the wooden bars into pastureland. Continue down the hollow until it bends right. Cross the stile in the fencing and continue to climb slightly left up the spur to a stile mid-field between elder and thorn. Continue in a similar direction through this next field, which is smattered with clumps of nettles. It must be the plentiful supply of slurry which encourages such prolific growth.

Kinver Church

You can see Kinver now, with the impressive red sandstone tower of Kinver church, thought to date from Norman times, and Kinver Edge beyond. The church of St Peter, perched on the hillside and aloof from the main village, would not have been so isolated in medieval times. The focus of the village has moved more towards the river and canal.

Cross the next stile and cut across, slightly left again, to a stile. Once through the path follows a hedge cum fence on the left along the bank to a stile by the main A449, opposite the Whittington Inn, the landmark you need to chart your way. This one time half-timbered manor house, is now a popular as a place of refreshment. Cross the road, and if you are not imbibing, go through the car-park to a lovely little path leading down to the canal. Come out on to the lane. You have a choice of return routes from here, both equally attractive. You can stay on this side of the canal by turning second right (not first – this is a private garden) along a clear path across a field, then rising through the woods and through private gardens to the track by Dunsley House once again. Turn left downhill and retrace your steps into Kinver.

Otherwise, go over the bridge and turn right on to the canal towpath and then left to Kinver. This is a beautifully tranquil stretch of the canal. You meet the road by the Vine. Retrace your steps into Kinver.

WALK 4: The Trent and Mersey

A short circular walk from the portals of the Harecastle Tunnels to Bathpool Park and Ravenscliffe. Easy walking mainly along paths with a small amount of road walking in Kidsgrove.

Distance: 3 miles (5.5km)

Time: Allow 1 hours

Map: Pathfinder Sheet SJ 85/95 Leek and Kidsgrove.

How To Get There:

By Car – Travel on the A34 or A50 to Kidsgrove. Follow signs to town centre. Car-parking available near to the railway station.

By Train – There is a regular daily service to Kidsgrove from Crewe, Manchester, and Stoke-on-Trent. Afternoons only on Sundays.

Refreshments and Accommodation: Available in Kidsgrove. Accommodation available throughout the Potteries.

Nearest Tourist Information: Stoke-on-Trent (01782) 284600.

Start from the railway station entrance. Turn right and pass by the signal box and down steps to the towpath. Bear right and see the Harecastle Tunnel portals. The one on the left is the more modern, being the relief tunnel engineered by Telford and built at breakneck speed within three years to be opened in 1827. The one on the right is Brindley's original, dating from 1777. Unfortunately, it subsided so much that it had to be closed to traffic in the early 1900s. When both were open they were used as one-way flows to speed up journeys.

'Legging' through Harecastle Tunnel

In the days of horse-drawn boats the boatmen would have had to 'leg' the boats through the entire length – 2880 yards in a tunnel 9 feet

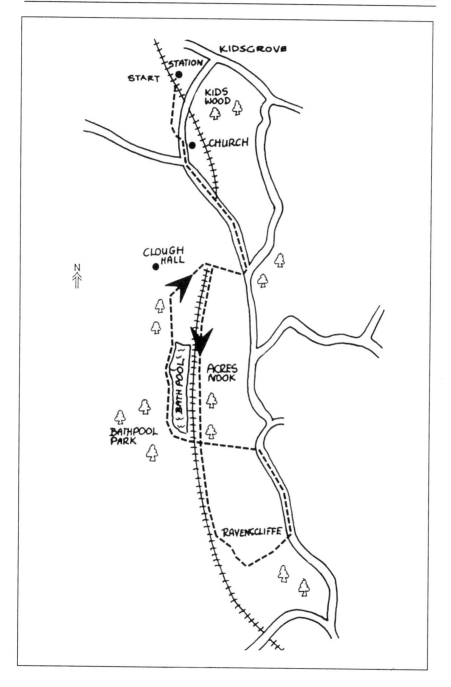

(3m) wide and 12 feet (4m) high – by lying on their backs and walking along the tunnel roof towards the emerging light: no easy task. At the same time the horses would be led over the hill to meet the boat at the other end. This walk follows a part of that overland route.

Walk to the right of Brindley's tunnel and continue up to the main road and cross over. Turn right and then left into Boathorse Road. This was one of the key routes used to take the horses over the hill to the southern portal. There's a lovely path parallel to the road on the right but you'll soon have to cross over to the left again. Turn right into Bathpool Park. You'll see the old railway cutting and tunnel to your right. This was the original Kidsgrove to Stoke section, which was closed to traffic in the 1960s. Walk through the car-park and continue ahead through the barred gate.

A Trainspotter's Walk

This is ideal for watching the trains go by, for this informal path within the park follows close to the track for most of its length. You'll see Bathpool Reservoir across the tracks, before you continue ahead along a more isolated section with picnic tables amid rougher ground. The path then dips down to meet a main track by the pasture. Follow this track for approximately 100 metres then turning left. Do not follow the track sloping left, but walk directly upwards through bushes to a stile hidden behind a patch of gorse. Cross over and climb up again, keeping to the left hand fence and passing by an old mining scar. It is quite a climb out of the valley.

Forgotten Hamlet

Cross the next stile and proceed to the barred gate. Go through it and turn left along an old track. Pass by a building on the right, which looks like a barn and was once a chapel. This collection of buildings is all that remains of the hamlet of Ravenscliffe, forgotten in the 20th century. As the road descends and begins to curve right, you'll see one of the airshafts of the tunnel and beyond the chimney of an early mill. There's also a good view on your left of the monument, known as Wedgwood's Monument, and to Mow Cop ahead in the distance.

A View of Monuments

Mow Cop looks, from a distance, like the remains of a real castle, but it is not. It is merely a folly dating from the 1750s, built to mark the boundary of the Rode Estate. In later years it became a meeting place for tens of thousands of Primitive Methodists enjoying collective worship at very large events with several thousand people attending at any one time. Near to it is the 'Old Man o' Mow', an unusual shaped block of stone, thought to resemble a human being.

Turn left into the green track leading down the hillside. Keep to the left of the hedge as the path dips down the hollow. A stile leads into the wood. You'll notice traces of the mining and spoil in the area, common to this part of North Staffordshire which was once part of a major coalfield. At the junction of paths below go straight ahead and cross the bridge over the railway to Bathpool Reservoir. Follow the path around the reservoir edge, then continue ahead up the valley by the games pitch to the car-park where you first entered the park. Retrace your steps to Kidsgrove.

Staffordshire Country Parks

There are a number of places throughout the county which have been developed for public access and enjoyment, mainly by the county council but also by other authorities and sometimes in partnership with private land owners. They are either designated as country parks or picnic places. The largest is Cannock Chase. Others such as Baggeridge in the south of the county or Park Hall in the north are extensive, but most of the parks and places have been planned on a smaller scale. They provide an opportunity to enjoy the countryside in completely different settings.

Ideal Starting Points

The four chosen for this section of the book illustrate how walking within and from country parks can be very pleasant. Most visitors tend to be content with short circular walks around the parks, so using these suggestions, you will soon get on to much quieter paths beyond the popular stretches. Most of the parks offer car-parking and often have picnic sites as well as some form of information point or centre.

Other Ideas

It is worth mentioning some of the other country parks or picnic areas, as you might also like to try walks from these. The footpath networks in these areas tend to be well maintained, making for easy going walks without obstruction. In the south of the county, not far from Baggeridge and near to Kinver is Highgate Common which is mainly open heathland with some woodland. It is not exceptionally good for circular walks though. In the north are a number of parks and picnic places near to the city of Stoke-on-Trent. Park Hall, for example, on the A520 offers short walks through an area which at one time was a major gravel works.

Further afield in the Churnet Valley, there are sites at Froghall and Oakamoor. There are marvellous walks along the Caldon Canal from Froghall Wharf, where you will find a superb restaurant in the lovingly restored warehouse. There are also afternoon trips in a horse-drawn narrowboat up to Consall Forge where the Black Lion pub is situated.

Until recently, this spot was virtually cut off to road access and even now is very isolated. Biddulph Country Park is also an ideal place for starting walks in the Biddulph area. Ladderedge near Leek also features extensive woodland.

Walking near Alstonefield

WALK 5: Baggeridge, Wombourne and Himley Park

An easy walk through parkland, farmland and along the former Wolverhampton Low Level to Kingswingford railway line, one of the Great Western Railway's later branches. There's some road walking in Wombourne and a shorter distance in Himley.

Distance: 7 miles (11 km)

Time: Allow 3 to 4 hours

Map: Pathfinder Sheet SO 89/99 Wolverhampton South.

How To Get There:

By Car – The entrance to the Park is on the A463 between Sedgley and Wombourne.

By Bus – There is a Wolverhampton to Sedgley bus which calls near to the Park.

Refreshments and Accommodation: Both are readily available in the Wombourne/Himley area. There's a tea rooms at Wombourne old railway station and several pubs on the walk.

Nearest Tourist Information: Dudley. Telephone (01384) 457494.

Start from the Visitor Centre at Baggeridge Country Park. Make your way along the entrance road back towards Gospel End, or choose one of the paths leading that way which will lead you to Point 15 where the bridleway crosses the road.

Point 14

Your target is Point 14, which is not that clear as there are paths all over the place! Follow the narrower path to the left of the road, up

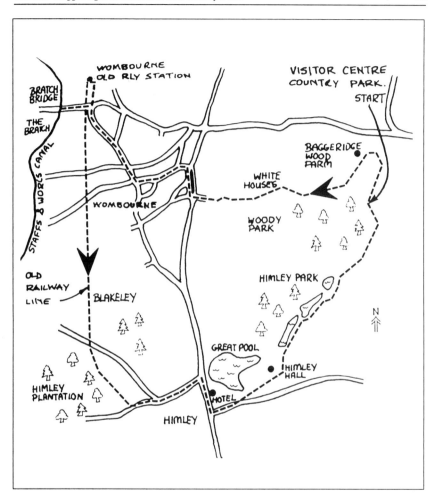

through the woods and when you meet a more distinct track turn left. This leads you to Point 14 in front of Baggeridge Wood Farm which is a key landmark. Just before the farmyard, there is a stile on the left. Go over it and join a track which begins to descend slowly. This is a fine section with pleasant views of both park and farmland in view. Where the tracks meet by the fields below the woodland, your way is directly ahead across the field, then entering a narrow strip of woodland. Go by the ruins known as the White Houses to a stile. Go over it and bear right, keeping to the hedge on your right. You can see Wombourne and the sound of the traffic on the A449 becomes louder.

The path leads to a barred gate by an old lodge. Pass by it and continue downwards to a stile by a barred gate onto the main road. Cross here with extreme care.

Wombourne

A little link path takes you down to the old road. Turn right then follow this to the bottom to pass by a pub. Just beyond it curves round left into Gilbert Lane. Follow this to the church and village green, a pleasant setting in this built up area. Turn right up Windmill Bank, go straight across at the junction and then take the second left, which is Station Road. At the bottom cross over Billy Buns Lane with care and then walk up to the old railway station.

The Bratch

If you are interested in a five minute diversion, turn left at Billy Buns Lane and have a look at the distinctive Bratch Locks. There's a picnic site nearby adjacent to the 'Victorian Gothic' pumping station. Retrace your steps back to Wombourne Old Station. The building and platform have been restored, and is now a tea rooms. Turn left by the tea rooms to join the trackbed. Go left and walk for about a mile through Wombourne, above the stream then under a road by way of a corrugated bridge.

The trail runs through a deep cutting to Himley Wood, now managed by the Woodland Trust and then, on reaching the car park go left down to the road and turn left to pass by Sandiacre Farm shop. Walk to the junction with the Wombourne by pass. Cross with care into a small cul de sac and continue ahead to School Road. Follow this to the main road. Cross over at the lights by the Dudley Arms, and turn right to pass by the handsome Himley House hotel. On reaching the crossroads turn left for Himley Park with Himley Church now on your left. There is a pedestrian entrance ahead at the magnificent gates. A Model Village is on the left with several miniature exhibits, including a railway.

The Hall itself is impressive and is currently being restored to become the National Glass Museum. Before you reach it, beyond the car-park, is a refreshments room and toilets which are open most days. As you approach the bridge leading to the Hall bear right alongside Ward House. Notice the old bear houses carved in to the cliff beyond the stream and pools. Follow this lane for a short while. As it bends to the left, go right over the stile with Island Pool now on your left and the golf course on the right. Continue ahead at the first fork, but then bear left at the next junction and climb up the series of paths, passing by the series of pools on your left.

Baggeridge was once an old colliery, but the 150 acres of derelict land have been reclaimed for leisure use. The brick works are still working and provide a contrast between industry and nature within close proximity.

The path eventually crosses a footbridge and curves upwards to a T-junction, where you turn right, and then up towards the brickworks and left, entering the green and the Visitor Centre beyond.

WALK 6: Cannock Chase – Moor's Gorse to Castle Ring

Comfortable walking mainly along forestry tracks with one or two steep climbs or descents.

Distance: 6 miles (9.5km)

Time: Allow 3 hours.

Map: Pathfinder Sheet SK 01/11 Rugeley and Lichfield North or Explorer Map Number 6, Cannock Chase and Chasewater.

How To Get There:

By Car – The starting point is on the A460 road between Hednesford and Rugeley at Moors Gorse, a lay by at grid reference.

By Bus – There is a regular bus from Birmingham and Rugeley, with a less frequent service from Wolverhampton.

Refreshments and Accommodation: There is a public house at Castle Ring, mid-way on the walk known as the Park Gate Inn. Accommodation is available in the Cannock area.

Nearest Tourist Information: Stafford. (01785) 40204.

Start at Moor's Gorse. From the car-parking area at the lay-by, go right over the wooden bar, then make sure you bear right to climb sharply and rising above the pumping station. The station contains a preserved steam-powered beam engine used in earlier times. Keep to the main path, avoiding turns to the left or right. You reach the summit after a fair haul. Pause awhile and savour the view.

Medieval Forest

Cannock Chase, in medieval times, was a very extensive hunting forest, thought to have stretched from the West Midlands to Tam-

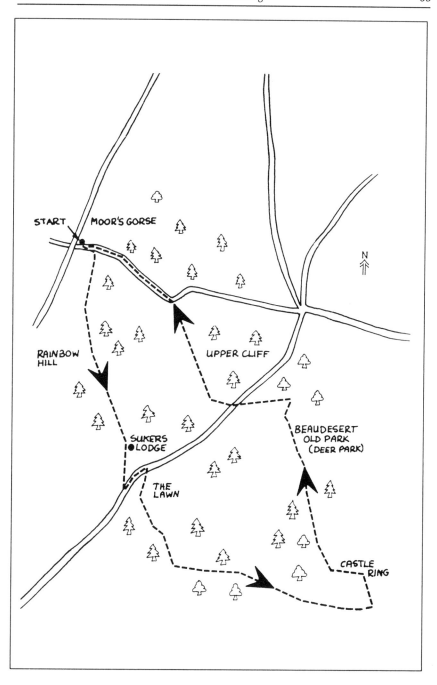

worth. Unlike the mass of coniferous plantation today, it would have been predominantly oak woodland rich in wildlife and game fit for kings and bishops. In the 16th century, however, this changed considerably with the exploitation of the ancient woods for charcoal burning. There was scant regard for the environment. Fortunately, despite the felling, charcoal burning, mining and iron-working, the Chase remains today as a designated Area of Outstanding Beauty and there are a number of sites of special scientific interest within its boundaries.

Proceed under the shade of the large pines ahead, where you'll see before you a white building, part of Beaudesert golf club here. Pass to the right of it and between greens to a crossroads of tracks, Keep ahead to the road below. Cross the road and bear left for the short walk alongside this fairly busy stretch. Take care. Opposite the car-park entrance, turn right down another forestry track. Once again, resist the temptation to turn left or right. The track descends, curves left and climbs a short while, before passing a pool on the right. At the next major junction as the path climbs, turn right. This leads slightly right through woodland to a major track by Park Lodge.

Go right to join Holly Hill Road and then left to climb up to the entrance and car park for Castle Ring. The Park Gate Inn is just to the right along a road. Otherwise go left through the car park to the earthworks.

Castle Ring

Castle Ring, built sometime between 500 BC and 43 AD, and no doubt the central point for an early Iron Age tribe, can still be clearly seen on the ground. The earthworks of ditches and banks situated at this high point is quite impressive. Defence was a prime consideration to Iron Age Man and you can see immediately what a judicious choice Castle Ring must have been in those times of outright tribal warfare.

After exploring the site keep ahead, but to the left of the earthworks. Cross a main track then continue ahead to join another track (or you might wish to go left and then next right). This is part of the Heart of England Way which runs through Staffordshire to Bourton-on-the-Water, some 100 miles, an unsung sort of trail which runs quietly through the West Midlands. Continue down the hillside of Stonepit Green to streams and pools in the heart of Beaudesert Old Park. The track then climbs up once again. Follow this until you almost reach the Rugeley Road. About 50 metres before go right and a track runs through to another junction where you go left up to the road again.

Go right and at the crossroads at Wandon cross the road and go left along Stile Cop Road but go left again along a main road. This is known as Marquis Drive and passes by buildings on the right. It then forks and you keep left and follow it round to the right by Seven Springs where a heron often sits at the edge of a pool here. The track bends right and descends to Moors Gorse.

Deer on Cannock Chase

WALK 7: Greenway Bank Country Park

Greenway to Knypersley Reservoir and the head of the River Trent. Delightful walking through a splendid country park and across fields on the return leg. One or two climbs, but otherwise easy going.

Distance: 2 miles (4km)

Time: Allow 1 hour

Map: Pathfinder Sheet SJ 85/95 Kidsgrove and Leek.

How To Get There:

By Car – Travel on the A527 from Tunstall to Biddulph. Signed from here. Alternatively, access can be made by way of Brown Edge, from where access is signed.

By Bus – There is a very regular service between Hanley and Newcastle to the turning for Greenway Bank, which requires a short distance of lane walking.

Refreshments and Accommodation: Refreshments are available in the Biddulph area.

Nearest Tourist Information: Leek. (01538) 381000.

From Greenway Bank car-park, go to the Information Centre and then pass by the toilets where there is a path to the left which takes you into the parkland and through two gates. Follow the path down the steps and turn left at the bottom. Follow the edge of Serpentine Pool around to the other side and then onwards again along the path signed to Gawton's Well. This is a delightful stretch through Knypersley Wood, keeping mainly within a stone's throw of the reservoirs all of the way around.

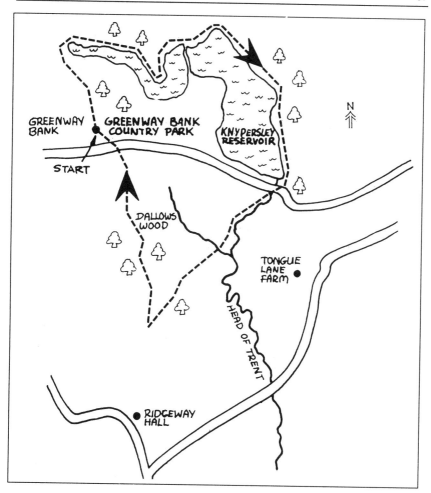

Greenway Bank

This is one of the most interesting country parks in the county. Much of the land was owned by two estates – Knypersley Hall and Greenway Bank. The first part of the walk takes you through what was once the gardens of Greenway Bank House, now demolished. This contrasts with the wilder woodlands of Knypersley Wood, a collection of oak, beech and chestnut mainly. It is exceptionally pleasant in Springtime when the anemones and bluebells flourish. The reservoirs were built later than the hall when the land was bought up by James Brindley's brother-in-law during the 1770s. He constructed both Serpentine and Knypersley to feed the Caldon Canal, which the latter still does.

Warder's Tower

Part way around you will come across Warder's Tower on your left and the footpath up to Gawton's Well and Stone. The Tower, dating from 1828, has been used as a dwelling for most of its existence and looks a tremendously cold place. You can, if you wish, follow the circular loop to the well and stone returning back to Warder's Tower. There's an unusual yarn told about both spots. The stone looks like a cromlech belonging to the ancients but was, in fact, the home for an 18th century hermit named Gawton and, being unwilling to resign himself to a slow and painful plague death, he is said to have cured himself miraculously by bathing in the water of the well.

From Warder's Tower, you follow a more prominent lane to Pool End Cottage. This once formed part of a carriage road, built for access to Biddulph Grange a few miles to the North. Biddulph Grange Gardens have been superbly restored by the National Trust. The 50 acre Victorian garden is something of a masterpiece. It was the pride of James Bateman who created a number of smaller gardens housing plants from different parts of the world, for example the Egyptian Gardens and Chinese Pagoda.

The main track reaches the road at the dam. Here you turn right for 50 paces before bearing left along a footpath signed to Norton Green. Go down the steep steps to the stile below, tiptoe gingerly over the sluice where there is a bridge. Walk down the dip to the right of the pool to a stile. Cross it and continue with hedge on left to a double stile. The main path leads off along the floodplain and you could well be tempted but this is not your way.

Head of the Trent

Is this really the head of the Trent? Thirty miles on it will be a swirling mass, a navigable water with some girth. Yet here, it bubbles as freshly as an upland stream. A few paces onward look for your path, which is far less distinct here, leading off right. It rises a contour between the oaks, then dips again to ford the brook. Once across, your way is ahead, over a bump and leading up to a stile beneath two large oaks. It curves left upwards again by the woodland's edge to a point where it meets a gap in a hedge. Then climb up in a similar direction through another gap in a hedge. Head for the stile before you in the corner of the field.

This is a meeting point of two paths, but do not cross the stile. Instead, turn around and head for the tree just to the right of the wooden fence. Maintaining this course, continue ahead down the hill towards Dallows Wood. It is difficult to see at first but you'll find a stile next to a barred gate leading into the wood. Cross it and follow the track around the clough and up to another stile by a barred gate. Cross it and bear slightly left joining a tree-lined fence. Continue ahead along the fence until you reach a barred gate leading on to the lane opposite the entrance to Greenway Bank Farm. Turn left and then right into the Country Park car park.

WALK 8: Jackson's Bank and Hoar Cross

Forest tracks, farmland and a small amount of road walking.

Distance: 3 miles (5.5km)

Time: Allow 2 hours

Map: Pathfinder Sheet SK 02/12 Abbots Bromley. Jackson's Bank is at GR 140232

How To Get There:

By Car – Travel by way of the A515 between Sudbury and Yoxall. There is a turning at Newchurch for Hoar Cross and Abbots Bromley.

By Bus – There is a very limited bus service on certain days of the week.

Refreshments and Accommodation: The Meynell Ingram Arms is nearby and there's also a pub at Newborough. There is bed and breakfast available in the area.

Nearest Tourist Information: Burton upon Trent (01283)516609/ 508589.

The walk starts at the Jackson's Bank car-park. Continue ahead into the wood, bearing right at the first main junction (300 metres) and right again at the next 100 metres past the benches. These paths are not dedicated as rights of ways, but have been opened up for public access by the Duchy of Lancaster. This wood once formed part of the Forest of Needwood, which like Cannock, was used mainly by landed gentry for hunting. The clearance of Needwood in previous centuries had not, however, been quite so dramatic as at Cannock. It was more of a piecemeal process in this part of the county. This is reflected in the present day land use. There are pockets of reasonably square and medium sized fields in some parts, and remnants of medieval woodlands in others. Most of the trees in this particular wood are coniferous,

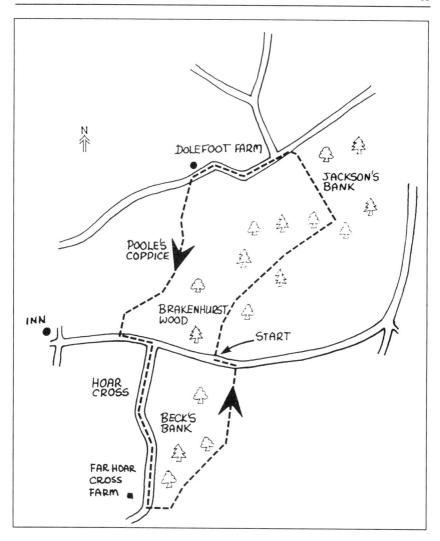

having been planted immediately after the last war. The track surfaces are unusual, being crushed gypsum quarried locally.

You will shortly see Newchurch church through the trees to your right. This brick-built church dates from 1809, evidently built for those who lost their rights in the forest when it was cleared and enclosed by hedges. It is one of the few remaining bonds, as a village never really grew up around it during the last century.

Timeless Setting

You will come to a crossing of tracks. Do not follow the red route down the steps but turn left and proceed to the barred gate. Go over the stile here and continue ahead to the footbridge. What a timeless setting. Once over the bridge you reach a tarmac lane. Bear left and follow this, ignoring the right turn, beyond the old post office, with the post box remaining in the garden, to Dole Foot Farm on your right. As the lane bends to the right, go left through the stile beside the barred gate with the hedge on your left. Continue ahead to and through a gateway beside a stream, still maintaining a direction ahead near to the hedge towards the white-gabled house.

Hoar Cross Hall

You'll see Hoar Cross Church in the distance. Considered to be one of the finest 19th century churches in the land, its tower is a significant landmark. It was built by Mrs Meynell Ingram as a memorial to her husband, who was to have shared the purpose built Hoar Cross Hall with her. This mansion, completed in 1871, was designed by Henry Clutton in a mock Elizabethan-style as the Meynell Ingrams wanted it. Their dream was to emulate their previous residence at Temple Newsam near Leeds in this gloriously secluded part of Staffordshire. The House is now a health spa.

As the field curves to the right and houses appear on your left, look out for a stile on the left at the bottom of a garden. Go over it and walk through the garden, with respect, to another stile beside a stream, leading on to the road. Turn left.

If you have had enough, continue up the lane to the car-park. If not, take the first turning right to Far Hoar Cross Farm. Close to the farm, as the lane turns right, go left up the rough road that leads once again into the Duchy of Lancaster woodlands. Once in the wood, take the first left and then, in 100 metres, a less distinct path right upwards. In 300 metres this meets another track. Turn left, then left again and leave the wood through the gateway. Continue ahead along the wood's edge to a gate leading to the tarmac lane. Turn left and then right into the car-park.

Famous Characters

Staffordshire is the home ground for many a celebrated character and in so many fields of distinction. Famous literary figures include Arnold Bennett, revered for his portrayal of life in the Potteries, Samuel Johnson, with his birthplace in Lichfield now established as the Birthplace Museum. Two literary scholars chosen for consideration in this section are George Eliot, a woman writing with great passion about a changing Victorian landscape and basing one of her novels on the north-west of Staffordshire, and Rudyard Kipling, a writer of a very different persuasion but also deeply concerned about the countryside, the latter, featured here because Rudyard Lake meant so much to his parents, the romantic attachment can only be understood by walking the more secluded paths overlooking the reservoir.

Scientists and Engineers

Staffordshire has also been home to great sea-going admirals, such as Lord Anson of Shugborough and Lord St Vincent of Meaford Hall, as well as distinguished scientists and engineers such as Erasmus Darwin and James Brindley. The latter has a museum devoted to his work in Leek and the first walk passes by this attraction known as Brindley's Mill.

Others, such as the landscape painter, Peter de Wint, and Josiah Wedgwood, potter and entrepreneur, are mentioned elsewhere. Looking up the associations of these and other famous characters is a consuming pastime, especially whilst walking paths through landscapes that they would have known well all those years ago.

WALK 9: Alstonefield, the River Manifold and Wetton

A taste of the White Peak at its best with enclosed fields, marvellous views and pretty peakland villages. Easy going with one or two climbs and descents.

Distance: 5 miles (9km)

Time: Allow 2 hours

Map: Outdoor Leisure 24: The White Peak.

How To Get There:

By Car – Travel on the B5053 between Bottom House (on the A523) and Newhaven on the A515. Take the turning at Hulme End for Alstonefield.

By Bus – Limited weekly service to Ashbourne and Leek.

Refreshments and Accommodation: There are inns and cafes in Alstonefield and Wetton. Bed and Breakfast available locally.

Nearest Tourist Information: Ashbourne. (01335) 343666.

The 'Compleat Angler' is known to fishermen throughout the world for its tips on coarse fishing rather than its description of rural life in the mid 17th century as witnessed by one of England's early literary figures, Izaak Walton. It is hard to believe that Walton, such an accomplished writer, made his way into public life from a very humble background in Stafford. He could be described as an early example of local boy made good, except that Walton achieved considerable business success in London without any formal education whatsoever. Even more staggering is that he lived to the ripe old age of 90, a remarkable achievement when life expectancy in those harsher times was half that figure, less for the poor, a little more for aristocracy.

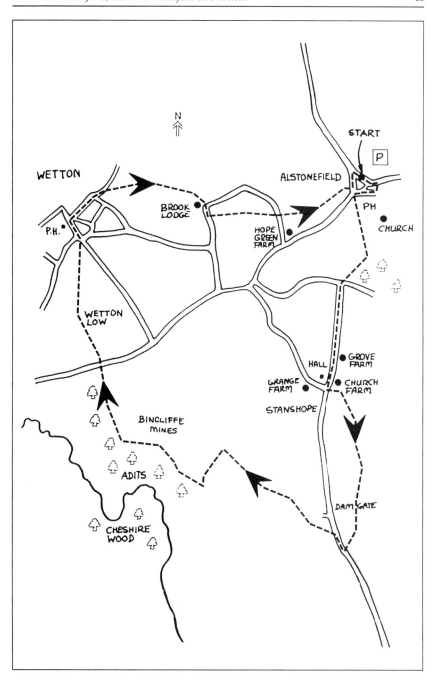

A Literary Talent

Within this time span Walton developed his literary talents and became increasingly devoted to religious matters. Fishing, without a doubt, was probably a very close third to these other pursuits! His great friend, Charles Cotton, himself an essayist and literary scholar, accompanied Walton on his regular sojourns to the banks of the Dove. The fishing lodge they used still remains in Beresford Dale, although the nearby home of Charles Cotton has gone.

Alstonefield Church

It is also known that Cotton and Walton worshipped together at St Peter's church at Alstonefield. The church, dating from Norman times but with 15th century additions, contains a number of fine box pews and a two-decker pulpit. Here, these devout Christians would join the congregation in regular worship, no doubt reflecting on the beauty of their natural surroundings.

Start at the car-park in Alstonefield. Turn right and follow the road to the left before turning right to the village green and the delightful George pub. Bear right again, passing by the post office and cafe. At the next road junction turn left and immediately left again along a walled track. (There's a footpath sign hidden beneath a lilac bush). There's a fine view of the church from here.

Drystone Walls

As the lane turns right, pass through the squeeze stile by the field gate and keep ahead with the drystone wall to your right. It is straight downwards at first, then funnel down to the field corner where there is a stile. Climb the stile and go downwards to the tarmac lane below, still keeping the wall to your right. Cross over the lane and continue ahead up a green lane, which will bring you to a triangular junction in front of Stanshope Hall.

Turn immediately left down a track signed for Milldale, and in a short distance there is a stile on the right signed to Dovedale. Cut across slightly left to a stile in the stone wall, then continue on the well-worn path to the next stile. Cross it and bear right almost immediately (200 metres) through a gap stile and walk upwards through a dry valley towards a ladder stile. Go over it and then bear right keeping the wall to your right. There's a wall stile which may be difficult to see at first, as it is beneath an ash tree. Climb it and continue diagonally upwards across the pasture to the stile in the corner. Upwards again, for 30 metres then right over the wood and stone stile, then walk diagonally across the field to the right-hand corner where a stile leads to the tarmac road.

Magnificent Views of the Manifold

Turn right and walk downhill to a point, just beyond the barred gates, where you'll see a stile on the left. Cross it and head diagonally across the field to the left of the farm. Climb another stile and turn right and go through the gate ahead with the farm now on your right. Bear slightly left with the drystone wall curving away from the farm. Follow this path to a small gate marked by a signpost. Go through it and, keeping the wall on your right, continue ahead along field boundaries until you come to a tall signpost situated before a track and a barred gate. Turn left here along the track towards Castern to a small gap stile beyond a rough patch and beside a metal gate. Go right and through a stile, keeping the drystone wall to your right. What magnificent views of the Manifold; to the left Throwley Hall, and slightly to the right, the spire of Grindon church like a beacon across the lonely hills. On your right the rough piles of stones mark the remains of Bincliffe lead mines.

This is a fine stretch of walking. Follow the well-worn path along the top of the wood, eventually moving away right, up a clough with a barn ahead on Wetton Low. Go through a gap stile. Continue up between the two walls before going left through another gap stile. Cross the lane, go through the gap stile up the bank with the wall to your left. Climb the stile ahead of you at the top of the field, with the barn to your left. Now Wetton village comes into sight.

Wetton Village

Bear slightly right, but keep to the left of the tree and trace the field path to the first of a series of squeeze stiles, which take you to a lane near the village centre. Bear right a few paces to the junction then turn left up the main street. The Royal Oak Inn is on your left at the village centre. Turn right at the junction here, heading for Hartington and Hulme End. Follow the main road to the edge of the village beyond Town End Farm. At the junction here look to the corner ahead, to locate a squeeze stile beside a field gate. Take this and descend gradually to the opposite bottom corner and a further stile beside a hawthorn.

Turn left over this stile and trace the hollow to a further stile, then go ahead to the far side of the pasture, to another squeeze stile to the right of a gate in the far wall. From here aim for the far right corner of the field to emerge onto an old lane. Turn right along this to the minor road.

Bear right along the road for 50 yards and take the signposted footpath on the left. Two further stiles in line lead to a further stile in a field corner. Climb this and turn left, heading uphill to a gap stile at a crossing of paths. Continue straight ahead here, continuing to climb to reach a lane some yards to the right of a small stone barn. Cross straight over and go through the squeeze stile opposite. In season there's a growth of gooseberry bushes here beside a small pond.

Continue uphill to the stile on the skyline and from here slightly right to the stile in the far right corner beneath a stand of sycamores. The roofs of Alstonefield now beckon ahead. Favour the right hand edge of this large pasture, the village sports field, and walk to the double gates near the far right corner. Pass through, walk to the lane and turn left along this to the junction. Turn right here to return to the village centre and the George Inn. Turn left again to return to the car park.

Staffordshire Walking

WALK 10: Ellastone and Stanton

Pleasant gentle countryside not frequented by many ramblers with one or two very wet sections but otherwise easy walking with a few climbs. Short quiet road section.

Distance: 6 miles (9.5km)

Time: Allow 3 hours

Map: Pathfinder Sheet SK 04/14 Ashbourne and the Churnet Valley.

How To Get There:

By Car — Travel on the B5032 from Ashbourne to Uttoxeter. There is a limited amount of parking near to the church and in lanes nearby.

By Bus — There is a limited bus service between Uttoxeter and Ashbourne.

Refreshments and Accommodation: There is a pub in the village and a limited amount of bed and breakfast accommodation throughout the area.

Nearest Tourist Information: Ashbourne. (01335) 343666.

George Eliot, or Marian Evans in real life, was a writer of distinction. She threw convention to the wind by living with a married man, George Lewes, and, unlike other literary giants of the last century, shunned all publicity. Her success can be accredited not only to her rich and sensitive writing, but also to the encouragement of her publisher, John Blackwood, who in the early years did not know the identity or sex of the author!

Marian Evans

Marian Evans spent a part of her life in the village of Ellastone, her father having been a carpenter here for some time. He is almost certainly the inspiration for the character, Adam Bede, in the book of the same title. Ellastone is 'Hayslope' and 'Loamshire' is Staffordshire. Many of the rural scenes described in this moral and tragic

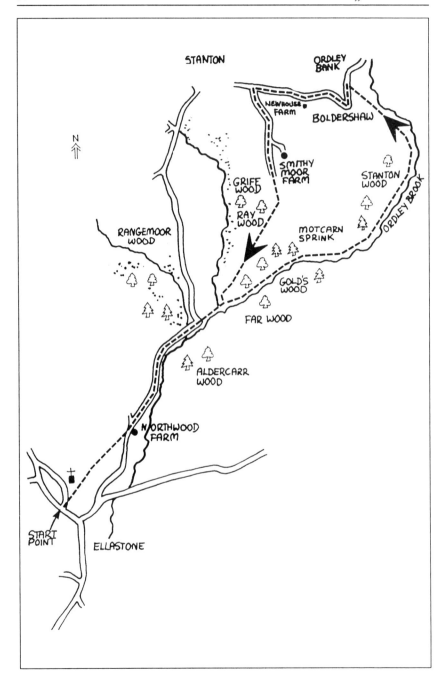

tale are sketched from memories of this enchanting part of the county. This walk could have been one of her favourites too. Standing in the churchyard and looking across the gentle slopes leading away from the village, little seems to have changed since this outstanding novel was first conceived. Read it and the walk will become so much more enjoyable.

Start from the church in Ellastone. Almost opposite the village hall, there's a little gate which leads in to the churchyard and the path takes you round to a kissing gate on the other side of the church. Go through the kissing gate and bear slightly left to a gap stile beneath an oak tree. Go through it and continue ahead to the next hedge where you'll find another gap stile. Go through it and the path dips down slightly right across an unrailed footbridge to the wood just to the left of the electric telegraph pole. Underneath the willows you'll find another gap stile. Go through it and your way is diagonally right towards the bungalow. There's a gap stile leading to the tarmac lane known as Ousley Lane. Turn left and follow the lane alongside Rangemoor Brook until the lane bears left and begins to rise sharply, just beyond a pretty stone built cottage on the left called Ousley Cross.

On the corner bear right through a rusty gate, (there is a footpath sign for Mayfield) and then continue ahead passing the remains of an old wagon and a group of hawthorns. A stream appears below you. Ford it and continue ahead through a lush meadow to a gate leading into Gold's Wood. The path is distinct at first, but becomes muddier and there are mini detours required to avoid the fallen branches and boggy stretches from time to time. It is sufficiently clear, however, to make a path ahead rising very gently through Stanton Wood with Ordley Brook always to your right. The path begins to curve left eventually, coming to a leaning stile, next to a broken gate. Continue ahead out of the wood with views of the conical Ellis Hill before you. The track becomes clearer and leads up to the tarmac lane, Stanton Lane.

Turn left here and climb steeply up Ordley Bank. Pass by Newhouse Farm and continue past the village nameboard for Stanton. In 300 yards, turn left down Honeywall Lane towards Smithy Moor Farm. At the bend where the farm comes into view, leave the tarred lane and go ahead down the rough track, past the metal gate and continue along the field road, with oaks, hawthorns, and a stone wall on your left. Trace the edge of several pastures, then go straight across the last field to the edge of the coniferous wood, and squeeze through the old stile, which is next to an old wooden gatepost at a fenced gap in the woodside wall. A tree-clogged pathway strikes ahead down the slope, soon becoming a sunken track. Follow this to the foot of the wood. Climb the stile and turn right to retrace the initial part of the walk back to Ellastone. See if you can spot the small dedication plaque to the Lucy Utting Memorial Woodland as you trace the lane – it's on your right!

WALK 11: Leek to Dieulacres Abbey and Back Hills

A walk mainly across fields, with a lesser amount of road walking. A few steep climbs or descents.

Distance: 5 miles (8km)

Time: Allow 2 hours

Map: Pathfinder Sheet SJ 85/95 Kidsgrove and Leek.

How To Get There:

By Car – Leek is served by main roads from Buxton, Macclesfield, Stoke and Stone. There is a large car-parking area in the Market Place.

By Bus – Leek is served by regular buses from Hanley, Longton and Stoke. Less frequent service from Buxton, Cheadle, Derby and Manchester.

Refreshments and Accommodation: Ample supply of both in Leek.

Nearest Tourist Information: Leek (01538) 381000.

Start from the Market Place and turn left towards the church of St Edward the Confessor, a church with a considerable history. Go right after the Church along Church Place and then drop down into Brough Park. On reaching the road turn left. This is Park Road and it drops down to a junction with Abbey Green Road. Go left here and right to follow Mill Street (A523 to Macclesfield) by Brindley Mill, a small restored corn mill sandwiched in between larger scale modern developments. The water-powered corn mill is thought to be the work of Brindley and bears an inscription: 'J.B. 1752'. This was one of many successful enterprises carried out by Brindley as a millwright before embarking on his extraordinarily successful career as a canal engineer.

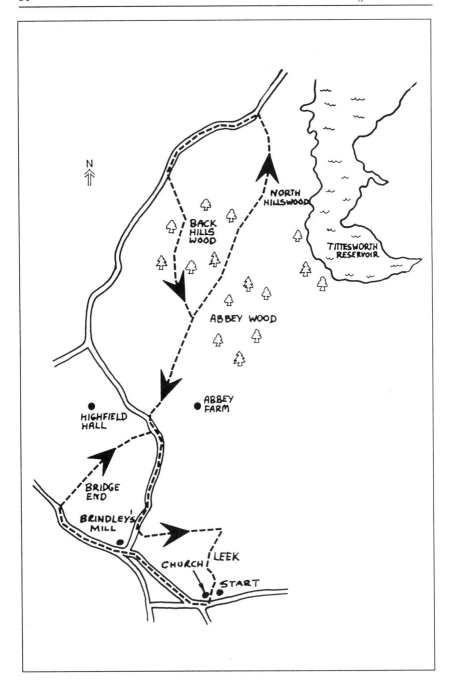

James Brindley

Brindley was engaged by the industrial magnate, the Duke of Bridgewater, to engineer the Worsley and Bridgewater canals near Manchester, but his real achievement came with the Trent and Mersey, also known as the Grand Trunk. The Harecastle Tunnel, the focus of attention in Walk 4, bears witness to his genius in the field. The Caldon Canal was his last, and to many, his most beautifully contoured navigation. It was literally the death of him, for after a soak-

ing in heavy showers while out surveying at Froghall he became seriously ill and died shortly afterwards.

The Mill has been developed as a museum, thanks to the hard work of the Brindley Mill Preservation Trust, which displays material about the life and work of Brindley. It is open to the public; there is a small entrance charge. Please check opening times before travelling.

Leek

Continue around the corner by the chemical works and turn right at Bridge End, a quiet corner of Leek. Bear right at the end of the works before a cottage. The path turns left and rises to a metal stile by a gate. Climb up the bank, with the hedge on your left, to a stile on your left. Before crossing, take a look at Leek. Unlike most other Staffordshire towns, Leek has a distinctly northern look; it is very much a Pennine community. It is not only the backcloth of the moorlands but also the compact, medieval nature of the town centre emanating from the church and market place. The town, like its neighbour, Macclesfield, grew as a market serving a distinct agricultural area but, during industrialisation, became shaped by silk production. The mills were not large and smaller scale weaving cottages and sheds grew up gradually around the medieval core. There are a few chimneys left and you can see quite clearly the church tower. Nearby is the interesting Nicholson Institute, built in 1884 as a public library and gallery. The architects were William Sugden and Son. During the 19th century they were responsible for many of the buildings in Leek, very notable in style.

Dieulacres Abbey

Climb the stile and turn right down field with the hedge now on your right. In the corner you come to a stile. Climb it, and then keep ahead to the left of the fence. Again climb an unusual stile. Head for the far right corner of the field with the cottages in the background. Keep to the left of the fence until you reach a stile by a water trough which you cross. Go through the gateway and proceed with the field boundary now on your left towards the cottages. Follow the fencing next to the access road to a stile. This brings you to Abbey Green lane where you turn left. As the lane begins to climb, bear right through the car park of the Abbey Green Inn. The name refers to the Cistercian Dieulacres Abbey dating from 1214; the scant remains are at Abbey Farm nearby. Originally situated in western Cheshire, the monks moved here to avoid the constant ransacking from the invading Welsh. They became powerful in this more peaceful area and would certainly have been influential in the development of Leek as a town. On more than one occasion it is chronicled that the peace-loving brothers turned pugnacious, joining for example, the mob following a murder at Leek Fair in 1516.

Fine Views

Go to the right of the red stone cottages by the pub to a stile. Cross it and head up the hillside on a well defined path to the top left hand side of the field. Cross the stile above Abbey Wood and follow the track ahead through rougher ground to the brow of Back Hills. The nearest landmark is the small plantation to your right. There are magnificent views from here of Leek, as well as the Roaches and Shutlingsloe ahead of you in the distance. There's also a glimpse of Tittesworth Reservoir in the foreground, built to supply water to early mills in the area and enlarged more recently. The path descends to a stone gap stile. Go through it and keep company with the wall to your right until the next stile by a barred gate is reached. North Hillswood Farm is before you, but, after climbing the stile, you bear slightly left across a muddy patch to join the lane. Turn left and follow this to a T-junction.

Turn left here and walk, facing the traffic, uphill to a house on the left, Folly Rest. Be vigilant here on two counts. The lane is surprisingly busy with cars. Secondly, it is easy to miss the stone steps stile in the wall. As the road descends cross the stile on the left and continue down the field, with fence, then later hedge, to your left. The path moves away slightly to the right to cross a bridge and then sharper right to a stile hidden behind a hollybush, which leads into the wood. The path, which is reasonably well-defined at this stage, winds its way upwards to the top right corner of the wood. It becomes less distinct towards the top, but you'll see the fields to your right as you approach the stile leading into the pasture above.

Climb the stile and walk ahead, beyond a holly shaped like a plum pudding, towards the line of trees slightly to your right. Follow the trees to the track. At this point turn right and retrace your steps to the Abbey Inn, which (rather conveniently) you have to pass by once again! Turn left on the lane and follow this back towards Leek, but, after you cross a stream, take the next road turning left. This becomes Park Road which takes you into Brough Park, through which you walked through on the outward leg. Take a right turning and follow the path up to Leek centre. The church is a good landmark to head for, but there are other exits.

WALK 12: Rudyard and Horton

Delightful, easy to follow walk through fields and along tracks, returning along the lake.

Distance: 3 miles (6km)

Time: Allow 2 hours

Map: Pathfinder Sheet SJ 85/95 Kidsgrove and Leek.

How To Get There:

By Car – Travel on the A523 Leek to Macclesfield road, then turn at Poolend on to the B5331 to Rudyard.

By Bus – There is a daily bus between Manchester and Derby, which calls at Poolend, a mile walk from Rudyard.

Refreshments and Accommodation: Both are available at Rudyard. The Crown Inn at Horton is a useful half way stop. It is not open on Monday lunch.

Nearest Tourist Information: Leek. (01538) 381000

Rudyard Kipling, the son of John Lockwood Kipling and Alice Mac-Donald, was a true product of the British Empire. Named affectionately after Rudyard simply because his parents enjoyed this place enormously in their youth, Kipling very rarely came north to see the countryside that so inspired his parents. Born in India and sent firstly to foster parents in Southsea and then later to school in *Westward Ho!*, Kipling had an unhappy childhood in England but his time in India was quite the opposite.

Kipling's links with the Staffordshire Moorlands, beyond parentage, seem tenuous. His parents travelled to India so that his father could take up a prestigious post, principal of an art school in Bombay. Life in the subcontinent seemed to have suited the entire family well and certainly contributed a wealth of material for the writing that was to

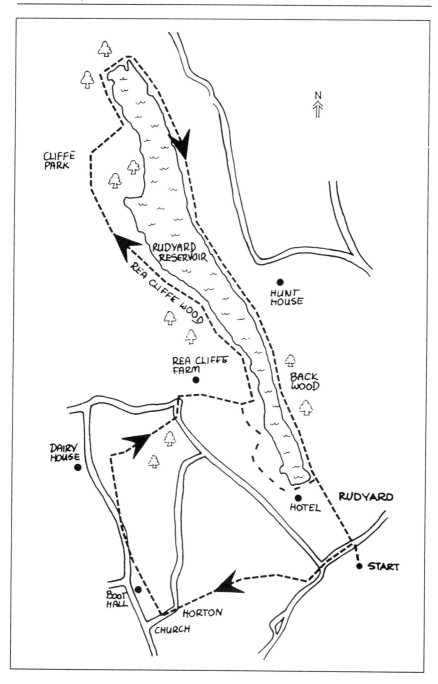

become acclaimed throughout the world by the time he was 30, including those children's classics, such as 'Kim' and 'The Jungle Book'.

A Different Era

The village of Rudyard reflects this era so well, the Victorian dwellings, the serene lake, the worldliness and charm of an age when values and attitudes were so very different from today; an orderly morality which is so embedded in Kipling's stories. The link is there in spirit. The monument in Rudyard commemorating the dead of three major wars illustrates the point. It begins with the Boer War, a struggle in which Kipling became intensely interested, then reflects on the First World War, which resulted in the meaningless death of his only son, and the Second World War, which Kipling predicted so bitterly in his poems and notes before his death in 1936.

But this walk is a reflection of joy rather than sadness, a characteristic of much of Kipling's work, which has been the delight of children at bedtime for decades. If you're taking a picnic today, make space for a copy of one of Kipling's stories in your bag for an after-lunch read to the family. The scene will not have changed much since the courting days of Kipling's parents.

Start at the car-park and picnic site on the old Churnet Valley Line off the B5331 south of the reservoir. Walk down to the main road and turn left for the short walk to Rudyard village. At the mini-roundabout by the Poacher's Tavern, cross over and walk up the track to the left of the Post Office. If you have a moment, take a look at the monument here erected by the parishioners of Horton to commemorate three previous wars starting with the Boer War, but also paying tribute to royalty during the past century.

Horton

As the track turns to the right, take a look back for the fine views of Gun Hill and the Roaches. The track leads up to a farm, but you continue straight ahead through two gap stiles to a field. Follow the drystone wall on your left as it bends left and descends to a stile and footbridge over a trickle of a stream. Cross both and continue ahead. The wall veers off to the left but you go ahead. This is perhaps one of the best views of Horton church and hamlet, an example of the rural idyll. Climb a stile and walk down the hillside to a gap stile by the gate leading to the lane. Turn left and walk up the sunken lane to the junction in Horton. Turn left here if you are to visit the church or the Crown pub.

Horton is a sleepy hamlet of real character, a few houses nestling on a hillside near to an idyllically situated church. It dates mainly from the middle ages but was restored by the famous Leek architect, Sugden, in the 19th century. In the churchyard lies the grave of a Staffordshire Moorlands poet, George Heath, renowned for sad poems, who died of a chill at an early age. Also in the churchyard is the grave of Mary Brooks, buried in 1787 at the age of 119. Perhaps, the monumental mason got his arithmetic wrong.

If you don't intend to visit the church, bear right immediately before the Old Vicarage, dating from 1753, passing several beautiful cottages and go through a gap stile. Walk along the narrow path for a short distance to another stile. Go ahead to cross a stile and you will find stepping stones across a muddy section just beyond it. Continue ahead for a short while, sweeping left to a stile under the sycamore tree. Once on the other side of the hedge, bear right and continue along a ridge of hawthorns with exhilarating views across to Lask Edge and Biddulph Moor. Climb another stile, then head slightly left through two gap stiles to a final stretch of path leading through bracken to a point where the track meets the road.

Turn right to walk up the track. As this veers to the right before the farmhouses, go straight ahead to the stile, then turn immediately right to climb another stile and proceed ahead once again. Continue over another three stiles and climb upwards on the path to a road, near to the school. Go left here and as the road bends sharply left continue ahead down Rea Cliffe Road towards the lake.

Walk most of the way down and 100 metres before it swings left you will see the Staffordshire way signs. You can decide whether to go for a much longer walk here or to return to Rudyard. If it is the latter, bear right along the path signed 'Staffordshire Way', through some undergrowth with a bungalow on the right. This path leads to a wider track running beneath tree cover. This bends right and as the track begins to climb keep to the lesser and lower path alongside the caravan site. Turn left at the junction and walk with caravans now to your left to a group of houses opposite a wood. This track becomes a lane in the village. Before the car park of the Rudyard Hotel take the path on the left leading down to the reservoir dam. Here you will see the steam boat which sails the lake and there are rowing boats for hire too. The steam boat takes about an hour. Walk to the other side of the dam where there are steps down to the old railway trackbed. Turn right and walk back to the car-park.

North Staffordshire Resort

If going for the longer walk, follow Reacliffe Road as it bends left and eases closer to the lake. This involves following the Staffordshire Way and it is very clearly defined, passing by the Boat Club then directly in front of Cliffe Park House. Continue on this track as it curves right through a large meadow to a road. This runs around the reed-fringed top end of the reservoir and then left to meet the old trackbed of the Churnet Valley Line. Turn right. Once belonging to the North Staffordshire Railway Company, this must have been one of the prettiest lines in Staffordshire. In its heyday, it would transport thousands from Leek coming for an afternoon stroll and tea at Rudyard, at the time a celebrated local resort. A North Staffordshire Railway Guide, dating from the turn of the century, comments that 'Rudyard is doubtless one of the best known holiday resorts in North Staffordshire'.

You will pass by the narrow gauge Rudyard Lake Railway and – if you've tired feet and it's running – why not take a ride along the last stretch back to the car-park? No doubt it is not as scintillating as the Churnet in its triumphant years, but fun nevertheless.

Great Attractions

Staffordshire contains some outstanding attractions for visitors, whether it be Alton Towers, Drayton Manor Park, Weston Hall and Park, Shugborough or Wedgwood. Their attractiveness is evidenced by the number of visitors passing through the turnstiles each year. There are so many firm favourites though and they can be found in all parts of the county. Consider Lichfield, for example, a city with ancient streets full of medieval, Tudor and Georgian houses. The magnificent English cathedral with its distinctive three spires, known as the Three Ladies of the Vale, is awe-inspiring. Virtually untouched by industrialisation, these precincts and homely haunts were once frequented by celebrated characters such as Erasmus Darwin, physician and scientist, David Garrick – actor of repute and Samuel Johnson, writer of distinction. There's a Darwin Walk and a Johnson Trail for those seeking a deeper insight into these former Lichfield residents.

English China

Further north there's a culture equally rich and rewarding, the six towns of Burslem, Fenton, Hanley, Longton, Stoke and Tunstall, known collectively as the City of Stoke-on-Trent. At one time, the towns were distinguished by hundreds of bottle kilns, factories and coal-mining, a scene of grime and smoke. Improved production techniques and a positive desire to improve the urban landscape is changing the Potteries, however.

Many of the potteries remain and the fine ceramics attract thousands of visitors every year. Not only do people want to visit the factory shops, but there is a rekindled interest in the industrial skills passed down from one generation to another and these are demonstrated well for us by a number of developing museums and attractions. The Gladstone Pottery Museum at Longton is a superb example- of a living museum where you can readily see and listen to how the potter went about his business in earlier times. The City Museum at Hanley has to have one of the most extensive collections of ceramics and each item unfolds a fascinating story.

For many though, the greatest attractions lie in the countryside, the natural features of beauty, the human made enclosed farm and parklands, the roads and tracks between outlying towns and villages. They all make for a great day out in the countryside.

The four attractions selected below are situated in the countryside and represent some of the more popular visitor destinations but do not let this stop you visiting the hundreds of other attractions in Staffordshire.

The Avenue, near Chillington Hall

WALK 13: Alton Towers

Alton Village to Alton Common returning by way of Dimmings Dale. A walk which climbs out of the village towards Bradley Moors, then across fields for a mile before returning by way of beautiful paths through woodland and steep sided valleys. Several climbs and muddy in places after rain.

Distance: 4 miles (6.5km)

Time: Allow 2 hours

Map: SK 04/14 Ashbourne and the Churnet Valley.

How To Get There:

By Car – Alton is on the B5031 from Rocester or the B5032 from Cheadle.

By Bus – There is a limited service between Uttoxeter and Cheadle.

Refreshments and Accommodation: There is ample provision of both in Alton especially out of high season. It can get busy.

Nearest Tourist Information: Leek. (01538) 381000

Alton Towers is not only a family favourite, but a first rate attraction which appeals to all age groups, for not only are the rides breath taking but so are the gardens too. There are fountains, streams and ponds, superb borders and terraces, not to mention the conservatories which bring out the gardener instinct in most of us. The garden furniture, mainly the work of two landscapers and architects, Allason and Abrahams, is delightful. The Chinese Pagoda Fountain, ornate and yet so functional, sends 70 foot of water towards the sky by means of gravity push, a prime example of this exquisite landscaping. The gardens are open for most of the year, unlike the other parts of the Leisure Park.

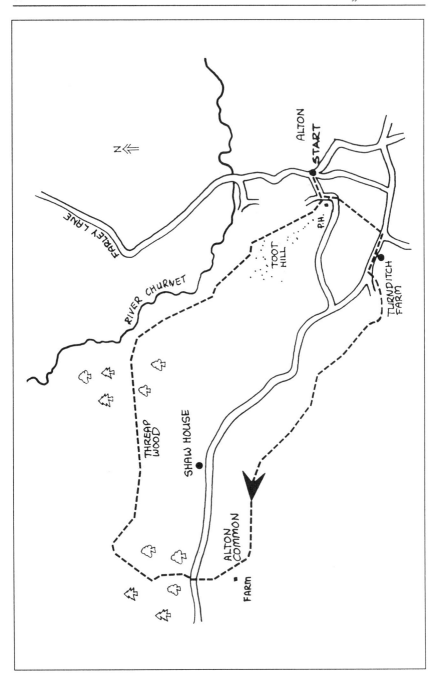

Earls of Shrewsbury

Previously, the Gothic-style house belonged to the Earls of Shrewsbury, but unfortunately it fell into ruins during earlier decades, the last straw being its use for military purposes during the Second World War. The interior was gutted, with only the romantic outline remaining. Restoration has continued and the entire facility is managed extremely well for our continual enjoyment. It has rightly earned its reputation as one of Europe's major leisure parks.

Romantic Setting

Nearby is the romantically situated village of Alton. The tightly compact settlement lying on the hillside of the Churnet is full of character. Overlooked by Alton Castle, now a convent school, you can easily see why this area has been dubbed 'The Little Rhineland of England'. Nearby is the parish church, dating mainly from the 14th century. Besides the welcoming inns and shops, there's also the famous Lock-up, a dome-shaped depository for naughty boys who needed to cool down or sleep it off. Not wishing to be disrespectful, but this is where your walk starts, a landmark you'll fail not to miss on your travels around the village.

Go down Knight Lane to the Royal Oak, then turn left. As this road bears right, up Cedarhill, you'll find a little path creeping off to the left over a wooden stile, by a cottage which has the lane name 'Cedarhill' in its garden wall. Take this path and follow it up the clough, with the stream on your left, up to a stile. Climb it and continue ahead again, with the hedge on your left, to a stile and steps down to the road. Turn right and follow the road for a short distance. Cross before it comes to the bend. There is a green lane to the left, opposite Broad View. Just before this is a footpath sign on your left. Take this, and walk parallel to the green lane.

Continue beyond the point where the green lane dies out, the upper of two hedges to your right. Trace this to a well hidden gap stile into the next field, keeping the hedge on your right, to a further stile. Once through this, bear slightly left to the far left corner of the large field. Go through the barred gate here and over the stile beyond, then head for the farm in the dip ahead. Take the stile just to the left of the telegraph pole and walk up the left edge of the pasture, passing by the farm and a bungalow. Beyond the end of the wire fence look for the stile beside the wooden field gate(left) then turn right along the driveway to the main road.

Dimmings Dale

Cross over carefully at this nasty bend and turn right. Almost immediately, there's a gap stile on your left. Go through it and cut across to
another gap stile, again continuing downhill towards the wood, where
there is a gap by an ancient wooden gate. Follow the well-trodden path
downwards until it meets a more prominent track. Turn right along
this, waymarked as part of the Moorlands Walk. This leads steeply
down to the mill pond. Turn left, then right along the path squeezed
between the two pools. Turn right again and continue down this path
with the stream flowing on your right. The path comes closer to the
stream as it curves into Dimmings Dale.

Cross over the footbridge here and up the bank on the other side of
the stream. Cross the track and bear right, up the stone steps, climbing
up to the stile. Go over it and continue ahead, with the wall to your
left and outcrops to your right. This path leads to a gate and then on
to a track passing by a lovely old cottage. Continue down the gravelled
road to the tarmac lane, turn right and at the U-bend go ahead beside
the National Trust sign, up the steep path into Toothill Wood. Once
past the rocky outcrops at the top of the wood, go through the pair of
stiles into a field. Bear slightly left to the stile and waymark posts. Turn
right along the narrow walled path then left with the Staffordshire
Way, following this back down into Alton Village to emerge beside the
Royal Oak pub. Walk back up to the Lock-up. Let's hope that you have
been orderly!

WALK 14: Shugborough and Cannock Chase

A walk through woodland and moors, with sightings of deer and other wildlife. One or two steep climbs and descents.

Distance: 5 miles (8km)

Time: Allow 3 hours

Map: Pathfinder Sheets SJ 82/92 Stafford and SJ 81/91 Cannock (North).

How To Get There:

By Car – Both Milford Common car-park and the entrance to Shugborough are off the A513 road between Rugeley and Stafford.

By Bus – There is a regular bus from Stafford and Tamworth.

Refreshments and Accommodation: There are refreshment facilities at Shugborough itself and surrounding Milford Common. Bed and Breakfast is available in the area.

Nearest Tourist Information: Stafford. (01785) 40204.

Shugborough owes its existence to one of England's most famous voyagers, Admiral George Anson. It was his wealth that created the buildings and landscaped parkland that is on show for us today. When he died in the early 1760s he passed on his fortune to his brother, Thomas Anson, a jovial character who happened to be a member of the Dilettanti Society, a lover of the finer arts. As a token of his love for his brother, he spent considerable sums on the house and park with the guidance of another lively character, James 'Athenian' Stuart. His nickname explains why there are numerous neo-Grecian monuments throughout the estate.

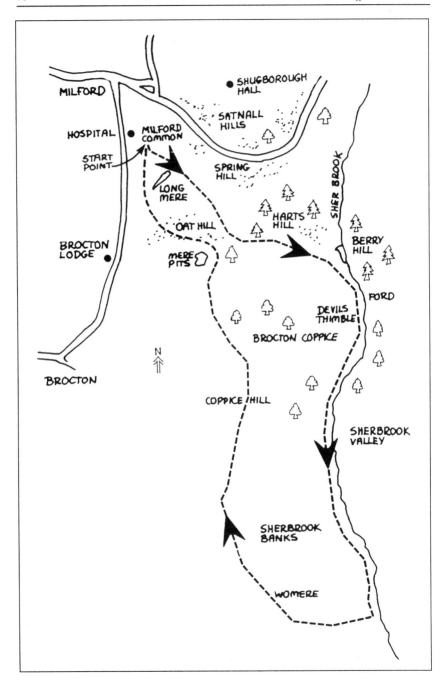

The Earls of Lichfield

Thomas Anson was succeeded by his sister's son, named George Anson, and during this period the famous architect, Samuel Wyatt, carried out further work on the mansion. In 1831, the owner became the 1st Earl of Lichfield and it is now the home of the 5th Earl of Lichfield, known as Patrick Lichfield, the internationally acclaimed photographer. The mansion contains collections of 18th century paintings, furniture, ceramics, etc. In the Park you will also see the Staffordshire County Museum information display cases where there are displays depicting the life of the servant in the last century, as well as a Victorian classroom, a brewhouse and a collection of horse-drawn vehicles in and around the hall itself.

Park Farm illustrates life on a traditional Staffordshire farm and there are demonstrations of butter and cheese-making, as well as several historic farm breeds. If you are looking for a shorter walk, there's an opportunity to look at the rivers Sow and Trent from the historic Essex Bridge and to stroll along the Trent and Mersey Canal. Otherwise, on leaving Shugborough, why not walk into completely different scenery as pleasant and interesting as Shugborough itself.

Milford Common

Start at the Information Board situated on Milford Common. Go slightly left and climb up the steps away from the car-park. Turn left at the first junction and left again by the mere. Once over the brow there's another dip with a larger mere to the right. Continue ahead up to the summit of Cat Hill, bear right where the track forks, then at the next junction continue downwards, the track running steeply to another junction in the valley. Bear left, then immediately right along a track signed to 'Stepping Stones'.

Sherbrook Valley

This is a section of the Sherbrook Valley, a serene setting beside the bubbling stream. Keep ahead and you'll soon come to a ford at a cross-roads, known as Stepping Stones. There are picnic tables in the vicinity, and if not busy, it is an ideal spot for a break.

The woodland begins to open up into moorland here and provides a refreshing contrast to the tree cover. There's a good chance of seeing the wild fallow deer and possibly rabbits or other mammals. In the woodland areas you'll probably come across a grey squirrel or two. Of all of these, the fallow deer are by far the most reserved, so silence can lead to closer observations.

Womere

Continue ahead once again at the is junction and the next one. Soon after the track begins to climb to more isolated ground and, as it makes a large U-bend, you turn right at the top of the U. Climb up the clough, ignoring all cross paths, and at the fork higher up bear right. This area is known as Womere, a very boggy area which is unusual in this part of England. Years ago the bog was thought to be bottomless, but don't fret, it's only a rumour. The ground does, however, become wetter and then you meet a wider path. Turn right. A trig point soon appears on your left. You might also see a glacial boulder on a pedestal, the boulder presumably came under its own steam, or ice rather, during the Great Ice Age.

Do not deviate from this path though. At the next junction, bear left towards the road but within a metre there's a path off to the right running parallel to the road. This soon joins a path coming in from the right. This in turn skirts a main path, then joins it. At this point cross the main path and at the corner of the plantation turn left and then right just before reaching the car-park. You enter woodland again, with numerous silver birch, and the path curves downwards gently and meets another track with white markers. Cross over this track and go downhill, across the next track and then climb up the bracken clad hillside, Coppice Hill, to another meeting of paths. Continue ahead upwards and then as a green appears on the left and a series of paths combine under a group of ancient oaks, the remains of the real 'Cank Forest', continue ahead once again.

The path begins to curve left gently and then descends at first before rising to meet another path. Turn right here and descend to a log gate. Bear left and first right down to Mere Pits where you'll see the mere on the left. Continue ahead and down an old trackbed, dating from the last war when there were a number of military camps throughout the Chase, some linked by rail. At the next log bar, bear right on to the main track which comes in from the left. Follow this back to Milford car-park.

WALK 15: Wedgwood, Barlaston Downs and the Trent and Mersey Canal

Mainly along clearly defined paths, a short section of road walking and a ramble along the Trent and Mersey Canal towpath. Easy going.

Distance: 6 miles (9.5km)

Time: Allow 3 hours

Map: Pathfinder Sheet SJ 83/93 Stone.

How To Get There:

By Car – Wedgwood Visitor Centre has a large visitor car-park for visitors only. It is signed from the A5005 between Stone and Longton or from the A34 between Stoke-on-Trent and Stone. For the walk, it is suggested that you start from the public car-park by Barlaston Green. The walk, however, is described from Wedgwood railway station for those using the train.

By Train – There is a limited service Mondays to Saturdays from Stafford and Stoke-on-Trent. The Visitor Centre is one minute's walk from the station platform.

Refreshments and Accommodation: There are pubs in Barlaston on the outward and return legs of the walk. If you are visiting the Wedgwood Visitor Centre, there is a refreshment lounge available. Bed and breakfast accommodation is available in the area.

Nearest Tourist Information: Stoke-on-Trent. (01782) 284600.

Josiah Wedgwood was a remarkable man. Not only was he a potter of distinction, renowned the world over for his new techniques and exquisite designs, he was a scientist and humanitarian. He also exhibited an amazing flair for marketing particularly on a international

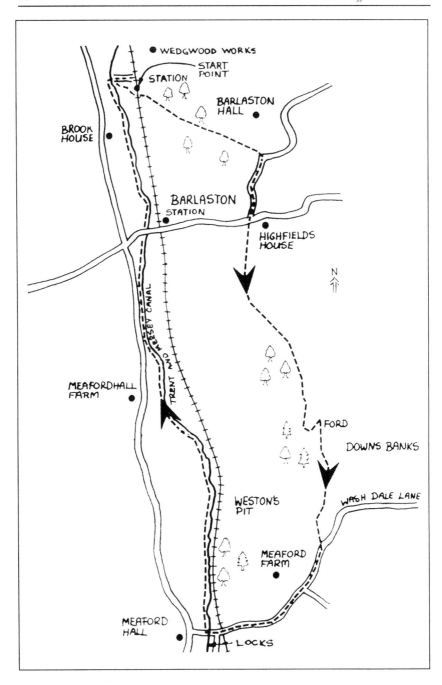

dimension. Despite personal tragedies such as the amputation of a leg and the death of his infant son, he maintained a direction in life which can only be admired. Born in Burslem in 1730, the youngest of 12, he worked his way through an apprenticeship then gained experience in a number of potteries before establishing his own major works at Etruria.

Josiah Wedgwood

Marketing Genius

He never missed a marketing trick. His success lay in producing high quality goods at a premium price for the elite who were so willing to set a fashion for a much wider audience to emulate. Queen's Ware was a classic example of this. Wedgwood traded on his image as Potter to Her Majesty, Queen Charlotte. In another way, his salient observations of human nature led to his philanthropic approach to his workforce and to the world in general. He was an avid supporter of the abolition of the slave trade and associated himself with other utilitarian concepts.

Wedgwood lived for work, always looking to solve technical or business problems. Hence his contact with other Staffordshire thinkers of the time, and the links with Brindley and canal building. The monuments to him throughout the area bear witness to society's gratitude for his legacy. The original statue in Winton Square opposite Stoke-on-Trent railway station is a timely reminder. Take a look at the next time you make the journey by rail.

Visitor Centre

The factory at Barlaston has been producing pottery since the early 1940s. The Visitor Centre welcomes casual visitors but please check opening times before travelling. The museum appeals very much, but people love to watch the skilled potters and decorators working in the Centre. There is an admission charge.

Start from Wedgwood railway station (unless you park at Barlaston and join the walk later). From the level crossing, end of the platform, bear left and just before approaching the narrow bridge over the Trent and Mersey canal there's a stile on the left. Cross it and walk slightly left across the field to the railway track. Go over the tracks with extreme care. Your way is ahead, slightly to the right of the wood. Cross the stile and walk the short distance to the green gate at the head of a pleasant pond. Go through the kissing gate and continue ahead upwards along a well-defined path over two stiles and another kissing gate before reaching the road at Barlaston.

Barlaston Hall

Barlaston Hall and church are to your left. The hall was built in the 1750s for a moneyed attorney from Leek, a Mr Thomas Mills. For many years it has stood empty. The church, while originally dating from the Middle Ages, was almost completely rebuilt in the 1880s. It contains a number of monuments to the Wedgwood family. If you want to take a closer look, turn left when you reach the road. If not, turn right and walk along the footpath past the pub and post office to the village green, characteristically at the opposite end of the community to the hall and church.

Barlaston Parkers Start Here

Cross over the main road and on your right is a car park and toilets. Go ahead towards Barton Land Welfare Home but after a few metres there's a kissing gate leading on the right. The path keeps close to the fence on the right and is well-trodden all of the way to Barlaston Downs also known as Downs Banks. Go through the next kissing gate to rougher pasture, then bear slightly left and head gently upwards to a track. Cross this and there's a stile next to the barred gate. Cross this stile and continue ahead over the bridge to another stile. There are good views over the Trent from here. You can see Tittensor Chase and Hill, with its monument to the Duke of Sutherland, as well as the cooling towers of Barlaston Power Station. Cross the stile into Downs Bank, land owned by the National Trust and of real interest. There are striking views of this secluded little valley from here and beyond lush Staffordshire farmland.

Continue ahead along the high level path at first. This eventually turns left into the valley and down some steps to a crossroad of paths. Turn right and follow the beautiful stream awhile until it comes to a ford. At the road turn right. This lane is fairly quiet, but there are one or two sharp corners, so be on the look out for cars. It takes you to Meaford Locks.

Pleasure Boats

It's a great pleasure looking at the boats coming through the locks during the long summer season. Bear right on to the towpath from the road and follow this past the remains of the one time awesome-looking power station towards Barlaston. There are shops and a pub in the village . If you want to cut the walk short, Barlaston railway station is only one minute from the canal. Furthermore, if you are returning to Barlaston car-park, go across the level crossing and there is a path alongside the road leading up to the green. If not, proceed along the towpath to Wedgwood. Your exit is Bridge Number 104. Retrace your steps to the railway station.

WALK 16: Weston Park and Brewood

Brewood to Chillington Avenue returning via the canal towpath to the village. An easy walk which is well defined on the ground mainly across fields and along the towpath.

Distance: 4 miles (6.5km)

Time: Allow 2 hours

Map: Pathfinder Sheet SJ 80/90 Wolverhampton North.

How To Get There:

By Car – Travel on the A449 between Stafford and Wolverhampton. The turn off is signed Brewood and Coven. There is limited on street car parking. Those visiting Weston first should travel on the A5.

By Bus – There is an hourly service from Wolverhampton to Brewood.

Refreshments and Accommodation: Both available in Brewood.

Nearest Tourist Information: Stafford. (01785) 40204 .

Weston Park, the home of the Earl and Countess of Bradford, is an excellent destination for a day's outing. It has a number of attractions, including special areas of interest for children. The House, the creation of Lady Wilbraham, dates from 1671. As a keen architect, she virtually designed it by herself. Visitors are able to see many of the treasures stored inside. Particularly special are the paintings by Holbein, Van Dyck, Bassano, Reynolds, Stubbs and Gainsborough. The Tapestry Room contains tapestries by the famous French Gobelin company.

Landscaped Gardens

The major feature of beauty for many visitors is the landscaped parkland. Staffordshire must surely be to the foremost in the preser-

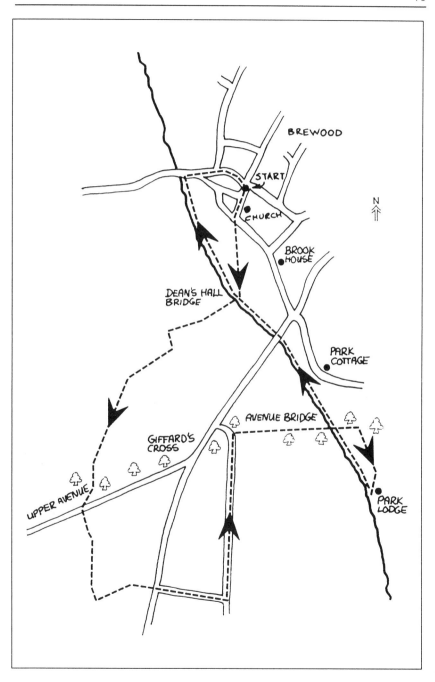

vation of garden monuments and follies. Weston alongside Chillington, Fisherwick, Ingestre, Himley, Tixall and Trentham have the inspiration and touch of one of the most talented landscape gardeners to have lived – Lancelot 'Capability' Brown. Working with him at Weston was Thomas Paine, an equally famous garden architect. Perhaps, the finest exhibits are the Roman Bridge and the Temple of Diana.

Rich in Parkland

This part of Staffordshire is rich in parkland and places of interest to visit. Just over the border in Shropshire is Boscobel House and nearby the Royal Oak where King Charles II hid with a trusty companion from Brewood, Colonel Carless. Down a quiet lane from Boscobel House is the secluded White Ladies Priory. Both of these attractions are near to Weston.

On this occasion, however, the suggested route is to Brewood for a walk towards Chillington Hall, which is also open to the public at certain times, and returning to the village by way of the Shropshire Union canal.

Brewood is a compact settlement nestled around the impressive looking church of St Chad with its very tall perpendicular spire, a landmark for miles. The square is full of interesting shops and pubs, particularly Speedwell Castle, said to have been built with the proceeds of a bet made on a horse of the same name. The walk starts in the village centre of Brewood by the Church of St Mary and St Chad. Walk along Church Road with the church on your left. Where you turn the corner to the left there's a walled path between two cottages on the opposite side. Walk this way to meet a track. Turn left, then immediately right over a stile into the field adjacent to the canal. Keep close to the hedge on your left, cross another stile and continue ahead on a well worn path up to the bridge over the Shropshire Union. Turn right and follow this track a short distance. Follow it as it bends left and then right to pass the front of Woolley Farm. This forms one of the most delightful sections of the Staffordshire Way and is clearly waymarked.

Chillington Hall

As the lane curves right go left over the stile then proceed ahead with the line of trees on your left. This leads to the Avenue. What a view of

Chillington Hall, standing solidly on slightly rising ground. Pause awhile to consider the life of aristocrats of previous centuries, a life of intrigue and indulgence, of exuberance and, in some instances, pretence. It must have been an uncomfortable existence at times though, for these houses were built for show. With rooms of such considerable dimensions not easy to heat to a level of comfort, many a lord must have spent a cold night in such palaces!

Cross over the Avenue and the road to a kissing gate. Go through it and continue ahead with the hedge to your left, moving away slightly to avoid the marshy area lying before the next stile, which brings you on to a track. This is where you part company with the Staffordshire Way once again. Turn left and walk up this secluded lane to a road. Cross with care and continue to the next junction where you turn left for a straight, but very quiet road section back to the Avenue, a continuation of a drive to Chillington, which happens to be in woodland here. Near to this point is Giffard's Cross, where folklore has it that way back in the 16th century Sir John Giffard saved a number of lives there by slaying an escaped panther with his crossbow.

The Avenue

At the tree line, turn right along the Avenue. You cross over the splendid Avenue Bridge where you can look down at the boats plying the canal. You'll soon obtain a different view of the bridge as the best perspective is from the canal.

After the bridge look for a narrower path on the right which cuts through the wood to the field hedge where you cross a stile. Keep ahead and at the next boundary you will see Chillington Bridge on the right. Do not go this way but instead cross a stile and continue ahead. Walk along the edge of the next field and you will see a dwelling to the left. There's a stile on the right allowing access to the towpath at Chillington Wharf. Turn right and begin the walk back to Brewood. Avenue Bridge soon comes into sight and you can now see it at its best. And all because the Giffard family at the time insisted that the canal should be kept out of sight as much as possible, hence the deep cutting and the very ornate bridge carrying the Avenue across this fine navigation.

The towpath takes you back to Dean's Hall Bridge which you crossed on the outward section. Retrace your steps into Brewood or return to the next bridge, where there is also access to the village.

Hill Country

If you are in search of real hills, then the Staffordshire Moorlands are for you. This southernly tip of the Pennines is ideal for those who enjoy the fresh breezes, the openness of the moorland, the patchwork of drystone walls and in places, dramatic outcrops. This is hard landscape to farm with harsh winters, none-too-fertile soils and a fair way to travel to market. Not surprisingly, sheep-rearing is the main pre occupation although the farming community is turning to less traditional activities to boost income. There is, for example, an excellent farm holiday group operating in the area, and activity breaks are becoming more popular.

Paths are quiet, besides Sundays, but even then you can find yourself traversing areas in splendid isolation. The Roaches is perhaps the busiest patch and deservedly so. Throughout the moorlands, however, you can soon find solace in the hills if you are willing to seek out the less popular haunts.

Not that the remainder of Staffordshire is entirely flat. There are groups of hills throughout the county, less impressive than the Moorlands perhaps, but, nevertheless, offering exhilarating climbs and superb viewpoints. They make for easier walking and offer different landscapes for the walker.

WALK 17: Hanchurch Hills

*A figure of eight walk from the Hanchurch Hills picnic site.
An easy walk along clear tracks and paths in and around
the forest.*

Distance: 4 miles (7 km)

Time: Allow 2 to 2 hours.

Maps: Pathfinder Sheets SJ 84/94 Stoke-on-Trent and SJ 83/93 Stone.

How To Get There:

By Car – Access is either by way of the A519 between Newcastle-under-Lyme and Eccleshall or the A51 by way of Stableford.

By Bus – No service available.

Refreshments and Accommodation: Refreshments are available near to the picnic site. Accommodation is available in Stone.

Nearest Tourist Information Stoke-on-Trent (01782) 284600

Start from the first car park (on the right). Look out for the dedication to the Right Honourable Lord Stafford. Passing left of this you'll see a rough road, known as Harley Thorne Lane, leading away from the car park. Follow this. Avoid the first turn to the right, go through the green gate, and pass by the reservoir then the countryside begins to open up. The scarp or steepest slope is to your left and you get glimpses only of the scenery beyond. The gentler dip slope is the focus of this part of the walk. Remain on this stony road until its end.

Forestry Paths

At the junction, bear right along the road. Do not turn right again into Harley Thorne House which is private. Continue along the road, which bends right to the house and farm. Here, go straight ahead down the rougher lane. Here there are splendid views south to The Wrekin and

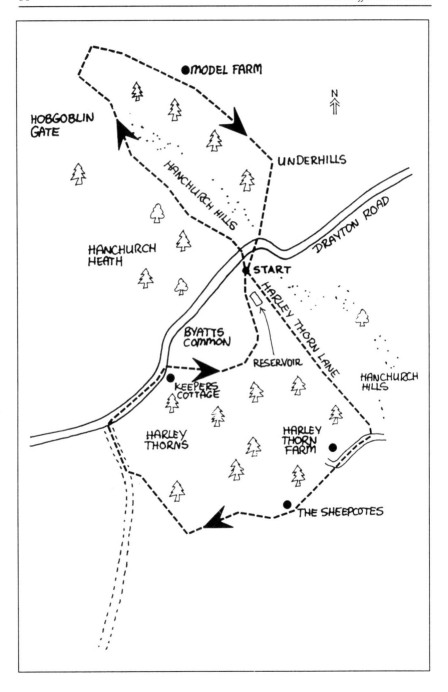

to The Long Mynd. You will come to a footpath sign and a stile into the wood on the right by ruined sheppers or "sheepcotes". This leads to a meeting of tracks. Bear left here, keeping to the perimeter path until you reach a barred gate and stile.

Follow this path across the natural hollow to Nursery Wood, where it soon meets a track coming in from the left. Bear right and you will shortly reach the tarmac road. Turn right and walk up the road to a point beyond the Keeper's House where there is a gate on the right. Follow the narrower middle track upwards, eventually reaching a field corner. Here bear left then fork right to reach a car park and picnic area before the reservoir where you turn left for the car-park.

Walk through it and cross the road. Your way is ahead along a wide forestry road. It is unfortunate that the conifers are so tall that they obscure the view across the Vale of Trent. Further into the woods, the way narrows and steepens, falling past agate to a junction of dirt roads at the wood's edge. Turn right and at the next junction right again. From this track you begin to see the scary slope of the Hanchurch Hills, a contrast to the gentle dip slope seen on the earlier part of the walk. As this track veers left, continue ahead to Underhills Farm. Beyond the buildings you'll see a stile next to a corral. Cross it and bear right up to the stile leading into woodland once again.

There is a fair climb uphill until you meet a main cross path. Continue ahead for a short distance to the tarmac road and the picnic site.

WALK 18: Kinver Edge

A short circular walk along this exceptionally beautiful edge, with extensive views of the Midlands and Welsh Borders. Some climbs but generally an easy walk.

Distance: 3 miles (5km)

Time: Allow 1 to 2 hours

For additional information on Kinver see Walk 3.

Kinver is a lively centre, rich in history and interest. For some years now, it has played host to visitors from the West Midlands and further afield wishing to visit the Edge, many of whom have failed to notice the attraction of the community. The village, particularly High Street, is worth a visit. It is steeped in history and this has been skilfully chronicled in a number of leaflets and booklets produced by interested local groups for our benefit. Take time to enjoy the village, its numerous inns, restaurants and shops before or after the walk. It will make your stay far more worthwhile. There are a series of leaflets outlining other walks in the area, which might also be of interest.

Crystal Glass

Begin the walk at High Street and, after passing the Plough and Arrow pub on the left, turn next left by the Old Plough. Turn first left again into Fairfield Drive, passing by Kinver Crystal Glass on the left. Continue up the steps leading to a tarmac lane, where you turn right, then almost immediately left into the Compa. Walk up to the lay-by, where your way is to the right, downhill to the clough, then climbing up once again along a main path very slightly to the right, which eventually becomes steps. This opens up into a grassy square. Nearby is Holy Austin Rock, thought to have been an early hermitage, and the rock houses which have been restored by the National Trust. These

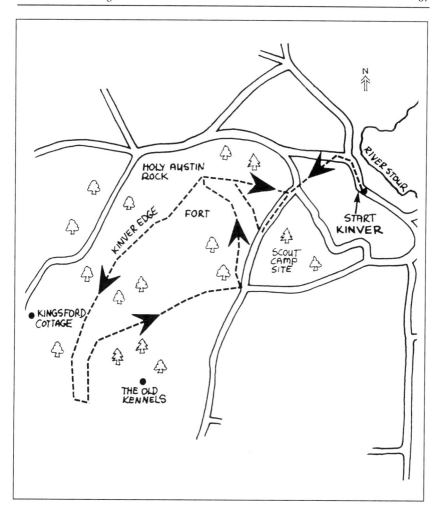

were once dwellings inhabited until the earlier decades of this century, some as late as the 1950s

Ancient Hillfort

Bear left up to the summit and site of an ancient hillfort. This Iron Age settlement was the centre of tribal activity in this area. The site is impressive. These hill dwellers would have easily been able to ward off intruders. Walk ahead, avoiding turns to the left or right. The views from the Edge are rewarding, across to Worcestershire, the Clee Hills and into Staffordshire. Take the higher path which continues ahead at first, then downhill to the right at the next junction. As the path dips and rises in succession, pass by a trig point and straight ahead once again. The path begins to curve to the left and falls gently to a junction of paths, the meeting place of the North Worcestershire Path and Staffordshire Way. Turn left here and left again at the next crossroads of paths. There's a gradual climb alongside a wire fence to your right. Turn right, now heading back towards Kinver village, woodland to your left and open fields to the right.

You come to a woodland shelter and open common. Bear left over the common. Once across this beautifully grassy section, used by many for recreation, there's a path climbing upwards. Follow this up to the ancient hillfort and retrace your steps back to Kinver.

High Street Kinver

WALK 19: Longnor and Crowdecote

A walk to the hamlet of Crowdecote in the Dove Valley, then climbing over the ridge into the Manifold valley and returning to Longnor. Easy to follow paths with one steep climb.

Distance: 3 miles (5km)

Time: Allow 1 hours

Map: Outdoor Leisure 24: The White Peak.

How To Get There:

By Car – Longnor is situated on the B5053, between Brierlow Bar and Bottom House.

By Bus – There is a limited service between Buxton and Longnor, and also a sparse link with Leek.

Refreshments and Accommodation: Both available in Longnor.

Nearest Tourist Information: Information is available in Longnor. Buxton: (01298) 25106 or Leek: (01538) 381000

Longnor lies between the Dove and the Manifold, a Staffordshire village of true character in gritstone hill country. Once a thriving market town, its splendid market hall is now a craft centre and cafe where you can see stone-carving, sculpture and pottery being produced throughout the day. On your way in, look out for the full table of tolls for the ancient market listed above the entrance. The village retains a certain attraction as a local centre. There are three inns (Cheshire Cheese, Crewe and Harpur Arms, Grapes and Horseshoe) serving good ale and food. There's also a fish and chip shop cum cafe

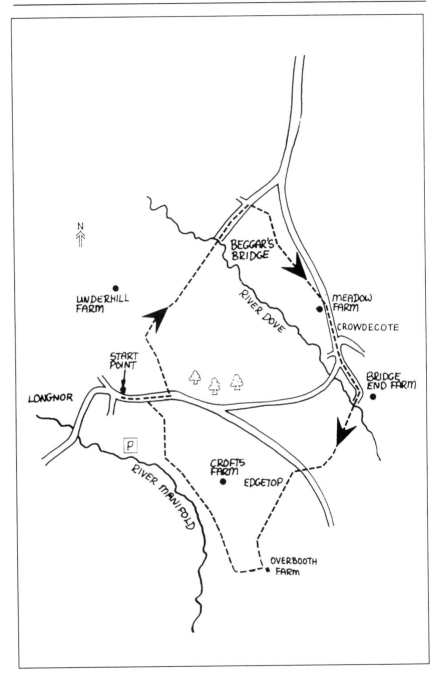

St Bartholomew's church is nearby and in the churchyard lies the grave of William Billinge who is said to have lived to the age of 112, which is surprising, since he spent a good deal of his life fighting battles for one cause or another.

From the Market Place, opposite the Crewe and Harpur Arms, bear left up the road to Town Head, passing by the Cheshire Cheese pub. Town Head is a group of cottages on the left opposite the entrance to Townhead Farm. Turn left at the end cottage, called appropriately Endun, and follow the road which runs ahead for about 200 metres to a point known as Top o' th' Edge; very apposite, for the views are magnificent. The Dove lies beneath in the valley and there are a number of hills before you – Hollins, Chrome, Parkhouse, Hitter, Aldery and High Wheeldon.

The farm is to your left and the road becomes a track which forks. Keep right to walk down the hillside. You see a sewerage works below on your right. Walk down to a barn, where the track swings right to the works. You keep left at the barn but next to it turn right through a gateway. A well-worn path leads off before you, at first rising to the brow, then bearing gently left to Beggar's Bridge across the Dove.

Step into Derbyshire

You are now in Derbyshire! The path ahead is clear following what must have been a much wider highway at one time. It leads to a gate and stile before a road. Cross the stile and then another immediately on the right. Walk ahead through a pasture to a step stile. Cross this and continue ahead, with a fence or hedge on your left. The path soon becomes a track, which takes you by a farm and into the hamlet of Crowdecote. Go right and then ahead at the main road, passing by the Packhorse public house. The name of the village most probably derives from the original Anglo-Saxon, meaning 'Cruda's Cot'. As the road bends right to descend towards a bridge, keep ahead along a No Through Road towards Bridge End Farm. At the fork before the farm, bear right and right again to a footbridge over the Dove and back into Staffordshire once more.

There are three ways indicated by arrows, Sheen to the left, Edge-tops in the centre and Longnor to the right. Your way is directly ahead to a hedge line dropping down the hillside before you. Climb up to the left of the hedge and trees which turns out to be the remains of an old track. You reach a stile which is not immediately noticeable. Once over bear left and then right through the hawthorns aiming for a the clump of trees on the horizon. It is quite a sharp ascent.

The stile is set in the wall just to the right of the farm. Cross it and the road to a barred gate. Go through the gate and keeping the wall and farm to your left, walk the short stretch ahead to a gap stile in the next field boundary. Now aim for the small farm building below just to your right. The path passes immediately to the left of the building and through the yard where there is a small gap stile before you. Please pass considerately. Go through it and continue ahead to another stile and then a barn. To your right is Crofts Farm across the field.

Pass to the left of the barn and proceed ahead to cross a wooden stile and a trickle of a stream. Go ahead to a gap stile and you will see Over Boothlow Farm. Aim for it, passing by a barn to your left. Cross a stone step stile into the outer enclosure of the farm then walk ahead to the footpath sign and then through the barred gate between barns into the main yard. Go right here and follow the track towards the River Manifold. About 100 metres before the bridge go right at a point where there are two old stiles by the trackside.

Walk ahead to a stile and then proceed through five pastures near to the infant Manifold. The path is well used. You will see Longnor to your right. The path bends right to a stile where the farmer specifically requests that you proceed single file. Head just to the right of the large barns. Cross a step stile here and bear slightly left to a metal gate by a much large one. Go through the yard and right up the access road into the village. Turn left for the market place, hopefully in time to enjoy some refreshment.

WALK 20: The Roaches

Along the Roaches Edge to Bearstone Rock, then on to Danebridge by way of Lud's Church. A walk along edges with weathered rocks and peat remnants. Paths with impressive views but some steep climbs and descents.

Distance: 9 miles (14km)

Time: Allow 3 to 4 hours

Map: Outdoor Leisure Series 24: The White Peak.

How To Get There:

By Car – Travel by way of the A53 between Buxton and Leek. There is a turning at Blackshaw Moor for Hen Cloud and the Roaches. There is limited roadside parking beneath the Roaches but please note that this now restricted. Congestion is so bad at weekends in the summer and on most Sundays there is a traffic restraint scheme in operation. The best bet is to park up at Tittesworth and catch the regular minibus up to the Roaches. This is proving increasingly popular with walkers and ramblers.

By Bus – There is a daily service between Hanley and Sheffield, which calls at Blackshaw Moor. There is a special minibus, mentioned above, which runs between Tittesworth and the Roaches.

Refreshments and Accommodation: There is a cafe at Upper Hulme and also at Tittesworth Reservoir and three pubs nearby, The Three Horseshoes at Blackshaw Moor, The Lazy Trout at Meerbrook and The Ship Inn at Wincle.

Nearest Tourist Information: Leek. (01538) 381000

From the lay-by on the road beneath the Roaches Edge make your way up the main path to Rockhall and left on to the Edge. There is a superb view of Hen Cloud from here. The path is very well-trodden and on some weekends you'll find yourself tripping over novice climbers

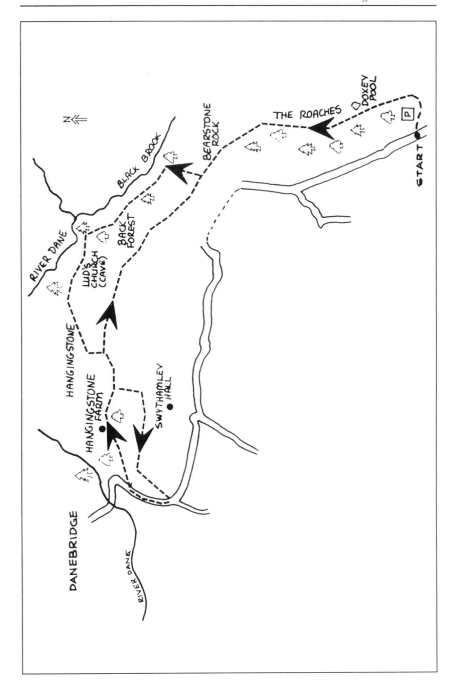

along this section. Your way up is waymarked and there are one or two steep climbs. Once along the edge, the crowds lessen but the views remain equally spectacular. On the right, you'll pass by Doxey Pool, reputedly never dry and the alleged home of a water sprite of terrifying appearance. Then proceed onwards to a trig point at 1,658 feet, where the descent to Bearstone Rocks begin.

Wild wallabies roam these moors, but you will be very fortunate if you see one. It is said that they escaped from a zoo at nearby Swythamley during the Second World War and took to the terrain and climate better than expected. Harsh winters and human activity has brought about their dwindling numbers in recent years.

Lud's Church

Cross the road, go through the gap stile and turn right again, going through another stile. The path leads down to Back Forest Wood. Once in the wood, it bears left and follows the wood's edge for some time. It begins to descend and penetrate deeper. There is no real warning as Lud's Church comes up on your left. This is a place of legend and mystery. The unusual name is probably derived from Walter de Ludauk, a follower of the religious reformer, John Wycliff, who suffered persecution in the reign of Richard II for holding services in this secluded spot. It is also said that to be the legendary 'Green Chapel' where Sir Gawain fought the Green Knight. It's a damp, cold, silent place, so it doesn't take much imagination to believe the tales. Look inside: the Green Knight's features are forever frozen in the rock.

From the entrance of the crevice continue ahead to meet another path. Ahead once again through bracken, bilberry and heather. You'll see a tower in the distance. This is no ancient monument, only a telecommunications tower on Croker Hill near Macclesfield.

Dane Bridge

Rise up to a gate, go through it and follow the well worn track ahead towards the Hanging Stone. Follow the track as it bears left, but then, at the walled edge of Swythamley Park, turn right and follow the boundary around to a property known as Snipe and then down the lane to the road. Turn right and follow this down to Dane Bridge. If you are stopping for refreshments, then the Ship Inn is not very far along this road in Cheshire. If not, retrace your steps the way you came a short distance and there is a signposted path on your left. Climb up the narrow, steep steps to the field and follow the well-trodden path left into the wood. Once clear of this section, continue ahead towards Hangingstone Farm and head for the left of the buildings. The path through is waymarked. Beyond the farm, bear right and soon you are retracing your steps to the gate beyond Hanging Stone. Follow this track.

Go through the gate and bear right on to the path marked to Roach End. There are once again excellent views along this stretch of Gradbach Mill turned Youth Hostel in the Dane Valley, Three Shires Head beyond (the meeting point of three counties and of early bands of robbers) Shutlingsloe standing majestically over the rounded hills. In the other direction, you can see Meerbrook and Tittesworth, Gun Hill, not to mention the Welsh hills on a clear day.

This path leads back to Bearstone Rocks. From here, retrace your steps along the edge to Rockhall and the car-park beneath.

The Roaches, Staffordshire Moorlands

Staffordshire Villages

The English village can be seen at its best in Staffordshire. There are still dozens of working villages not totally dominated by dormitory accommodation. They also exhibit many of the features we would ascribe to the classic rural community – the green, the coaching inn set in the square, distinctive features of antiquity, including those medieval church spires and towers which can be seen from miles around. In some instances, there's also the survival of ancient customs, such as the Horn Dance of Abbots Bromley or the Well Dressing at Endon. Add to this the multitude of annual carnivals, fairs and fetes and you have the very best in village life.

Gradual Development

Staffordshire villages tell a story of gradual development over the centuries, of land ownership and how this has often shaped the layout of a settlement. It is very much about family ties which have been passed down from generation to generation and of changing economic circumstances. Gone are the wind or water mills, the water troughs for the animals, the brewhouse or bakery. They are rare finds these days. Nevertheless, so much of the fabric of the village remains and, despite the changes of architecture, the streets have altered little over the centuries. Several observers of rural life fear that recent trends could bring about a threat to villages which would be hard to accept. They cite the closure of shops, the closure of pubs by the larger breweries, redundant churches and the decline of the country bus as factors which will eventually lead to villages becoming soulless places.

Regeneration

Rural regeneration is a process being pursued by many of the communities. This section includes ten villages which are very different in character and size. But one factor they have in common is a community spirit and a willingness to build on what the village has to offer, not only for the villager but also for the visitor. After all, every penny spent in local shops, inns, garages or buses adds to the maintenance of local employment in the community. Staffordshire villages are meeting this opportunity in different ways. Hopefully, they will offer a warm welcome to the would-be walker savouring local attractions and places of interest, not to mention some of Staffordshire's loveliest countryside.

WALK 21: Abbots Bromley

A short ramble along a section of the Staffordshire Way returning through farming country. Easy walking.

Distance: 2 miles (4km)

Time: Allow 1 hour

Map: Pathfinder Sheet 02/12 Abbotts Bromley.

How To Get There:

By Car – Abbots Bromley is situated on the B5014 from Handsacre, which meets the B5013 from Uttoxeter. The B5017 allows access from Burton-on-Trent

By Bus – There is an irregular service from Rugeley.

Refreshments and Accommodation: There is a plentiful supply in the village.

Nearest Tourist Information: Burton-on-Trent. (01283) 516609.

Abbots Bromley is a lovely old settlement of some size. The ancient Butter Cross is a distinctive feature, but by no means the only feature of historical interest in the village! The annual Horn Dance, held here every September, is a fascinating ritual thought to have either been originally a fertility dance or a celebration of hunting rights in the Forest of Needwood. The dance lasts all day and takes in dozens of farms in a 20 mile circuit, a gruelling exercise for the participants dressed as Maid Marion, Hobby Horse, etc. Thankfully, they receive beverages to fortify them on their journey. The walk outlined here is far less rigorous!

The Church

Start from the Butter Cross and walk down the street in front of the Goats Head Inn to the churchyard. Continue beyond the church (to

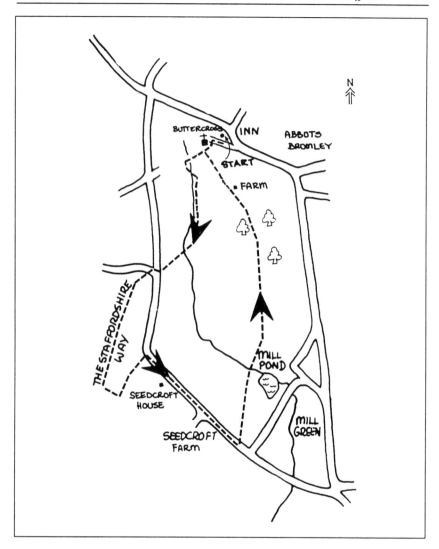

your right), which dates from medieval times but has much 19th century restoration. Go to the far south west corner, cross the stream and in 50 metres there is access on your left to the meadow. This forms part of the Staffordshire Way and is waymarked with an arrow. Walk down the field gradually towards the stream. There is a footbridge crossing it. Then go over the stile and bear right. As this lane veers right over a cattle-grid, continue through the squeeze stile ahead along a field road to another gate where you turn sharp right. In a short distance, turn left over the stile and walk up this gentle slope.

Blithfield Reservoir

Cross another stile and soon the expanse of Blithfield Reservoir appears before you. Continue ahead to another stile. In the next field your way is down an avenue of trees to another stile where you bear left along a green lane. You soon reach a tarmac lane and this is where you part company with the Staffordshire Way.

Turn left and at the next junction right. Walk along this quiet lane beyond Seedcroft Farm (not House), and soon a well hidden stile with a path signed to Abbots Bromley will appear on the left. Climb the stile and go half-left, keeping to the right of the pool situated mid-field. The exit from this field is not immediately obvious, but will be found slightly to the right of the left-hand corner. Go over the footbridge and keep to the hedge on your right. In the corner of the field, a stile leads you through the hedge to the adjacent field. Bear left and follow this up towards a higher level field, keeping the hedge on your left. Climb up and continue ahead with the hedge still on your left, school fields to your right.

Climb over the stile and walk along the rough lane to a junction. Go over the stile opposite and skirt around the farm (off to your right). Head downhill to a stile, leading into the churchyard and retrace your steps to the Butter Cross.

WALK 22: Clifton Camprille

A short circular walk from this small village in the very eastern tip of the county. An easy walk mainly along field hedges, with a small amount of road walking.

Distance: 2.5 miles (5km)

Time: Allow 1 hour.

Map: Pathfinder Sheets SK 21/31 Ashby de la Zouch and SK 20/30 Tamworth.

How To Get There:

By Car – Travel on the A419 from Tamworth and take the turning for Thorpe Constantine and Clifton Campville. From Lichfield take the road to Whittington and Elford, crossing the A513 to continue to Harlaston and Haunton. There is limited street parking available in Clifton.

By Bus – There is a limited bus service from Tamworth.

Refreshments and Accommodation: There is a pub, The Green Man, in the village and in nearby communities. Very limited accommodation available.

Nearest Tourist Information: Lichfield. (01543) 252109 Tamworth. (01827) 59134.

Clifton Campville is a pleasant little village lying close to the boundaries of three counties. This is a flat land of arable farming, grubbed up hedges and quiet lanes. It is not well recognised walking territory and many of the paths suffer as a result, often with overgrowth and obstructions. Nevertheless, a visit to Clifton Campville is worthwhile if you intend to take a break between a visit to Lichfield and Tamworth.

The walk is longer than in the first edition of the book as more paths have been opened in the parish in the past 10 years.

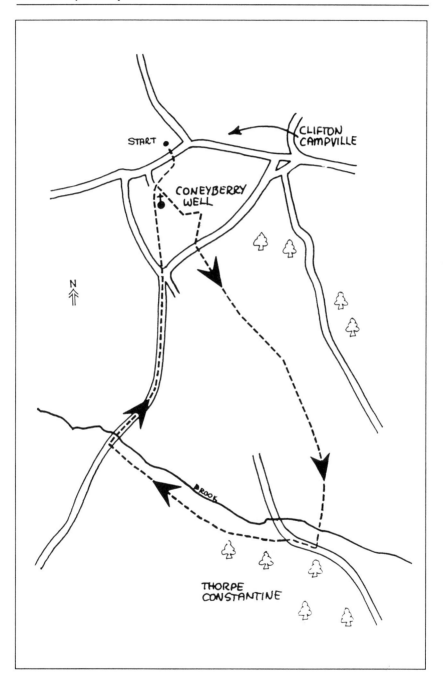

Distinctive Spire

Start in Church Street and walk up to the church gate. The setting is delightful, a magnificent church before you, with country cottages and a vicarage enhancing the approach. Throughout the walk you'll see the tall and slender spire of Clifton Campville church reaching to the sky against the flat landscape. If time permits take a look inside. Of particular interest are the monuments to landed gentry of earlier centuries, obviously benefactors of the church, very large now for what is today a relatively small village.

Start from the Green Man public house. Go right along Main Street and then turn first left into St David's Road. This is a cul de sac. Turn left into St Andrew's Close and look for a little path between gardens on the right. There is a thread of paths across this meadow as many locals take their dogs for a walk here. Head slightly left of the church and you need to aim for a stile in the far corner by a gate. This leads to a road.

Cross over the road with care. Go over a stile by a gate into a field. Continue ahead along a slightly raised track and onward to the next stile. Go ahead once again to cross a green track. The hedge has obviously been grubbed here. Maintain a steady path ahead once again.

In the distance is the church spire of Thorpe Constantine, a name which reflects a Scandinavian origin. This is thought to have been a much larger settlement in the Middle Ages, but for a number of reasons became one of the deserted villages of England. Next to Thorpe Hall, for example, is a lovely little chapel dating from these times, not built especially for the pretentious looking Georgian House alongside. It begs the question why Clifton Campville survived and Thorpe Constantine withered?

You come to a gap in a hedge. Go through it and the path now descends slightly right. Go through another gap and now drop to a bridge over a small stream. Walk through the woodland belt to a stile. Then head slightly right up the field to a gateway to the right of a dwelling. Go left to take a look at the hall or right if returning to Clifton Campville.

At the corner, before reaching the bridge, go through a barred gate on the left. Leave the farm track and head slightly right over the field to a very tidy hedge. Cross a stile here. Proceed ahead, once again, with the stream to your right to a hedge, but to cross another stile at present into a plantation. The path winds through to another field and continues ahead by the stream to a lane. From here, you turn right and follow it to the crossroads.

Cross the junction of roads with the church before you. You will see a stile leading into the field. Head for the church and there is a stile providing access to the churchyard. Retrace your steps into the village.

WALK 23: Eccleshall, Pershall and Cop Mere

An easy walk along clear paths but with some lane walking.

Distance: 6 miles (9.5km)

Time: Allow 3 hours

Maps: Pathfinder sheets SJ 82/92 Stafford and SJ 62/72 Hodnet and Norbury. A very short distance is on a third map sheet SJ 63/73 Market Drayton.

How To Get There:

By Car – Eccleshall is on the A519 from Stoke-on-Trent and the A5013 from Stafford. There is a public car-parking area in Eccleshall.

By Bus – There is a bus service from Stafford and a less frequent route via Stone.

Refreshments and Accommodation: There is an ample supply of both in Eccleshall.

Nearest Tourist Information: Stafford. (01785) 40204.

Eccleshall was once the home of the Bishops of Lichfield and indeed five sleep now in the distinguished parish church. At one time this settlement became important as a market town and was granted a charter to hold a weekly market. The High Street looks the part and it is reckoned that the arcades belonging to the Crown and the Royal Oak inns once sheltered many a street trader, selling his or her wares. This is an impressive street with shops and fine Georgian houses. It combines an unusual mixture of styles. The old fire station, for example, has been recently renovated and is now a hairdresser's salon.

Eccleshall Castle

Nearby is Eccleshall Castle which dates from the middle ages. It was once the home of the Bishops of Richfield, but is now a private residence open to the public at certain times. A few miles away is Izaak Walton's Cottage at Shallowford, which is also open to visitors. This makes Eccleshall an attractive place to visit, but don't forget to step out into one of the loveliest parts of the county.

Start from the High Street in Eccleshall. Pass by Holy Trinity Church and Kerry Lane comes up shortly on your left. Look for the mossy path between two gardens. As you enter the field, your way is confirmed by a directional sign to Cop Mere and Elford Heath. Walk up the bank to wards the electricity transmission pole and then head upwards slightly left to a hedge, where the stile is to the left of a small plantation. Cross the stile and enter a very large field. Bear right and maintain a path ahead, rather than following the convoluted field boundary exactly. You come to a gate. The view is beautiful and you can see Cop Mere in the distance. Maintain a path ahead to a small gate mid-field. Go through it and proceed downhill to the far left corner.

Climb over the gate and then bear right immediately past the chevron. Climb the stile and bear slightly left for the short distance to another stile. Climb it and then bear right diagonally across the field to a stile in the far left-hand corner. Cross the stile and turn right. This tarmac lane leads to Pershall, where you turn left. Continue, and as the road turns right by a cottage go through the gate ahead and proceed across this field to the left of the electric telegraph poles, heading for the large oak. The map indicates that there should be access to the lane just to your right here, but the nearest diversion is to cross by the oak and continue a short distance ahead to a gate leading on to a tarmac lane. Turn left here and, after a short while, the road bends and Cop Mere appears on the right. Walk around the corner and there is a ladder stile on the right.

Cop Mere

Climb the stile and follow the well-trodden path along a hedge on your left. This does not spoil the views, however. Cross over the stile by a gate on the left and continue to follow the hedge. Go over a stile and pass by a delightful stream and pond. Cross over another stile into the next field. Bear left and follow the field boundary to the next stile. Climb it and follow the fence, left, to a further stile into woods. Walk

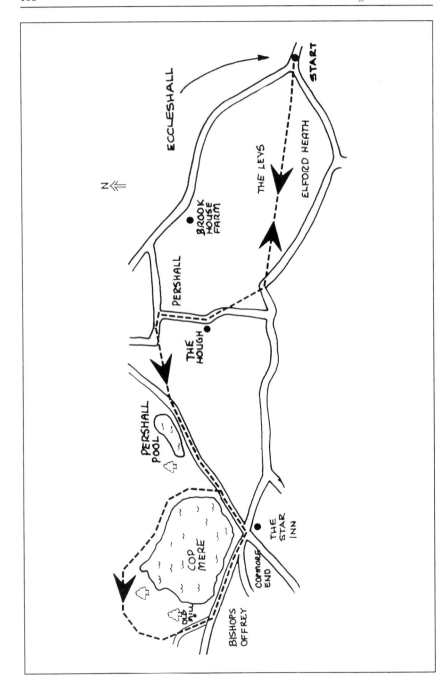

straight ahead through the woodland edge and into the field beyond. Your path is ahead now, keeping the hedge to your right. The village of Offley appears on your left and at the head of the next long, thin field is the remains of an old mill. Come out at the gateway onto a road alongside the impressive wall of what was once presumably the mill owner's house.

Turn left and walk by the mill pond. Turn left again and walk through the hamlet known as Walk Mill to the Star Inn, a most interesting public house. At the road junction, bear left again towards Pershall and retrace your steps back to Eccleshall.

WALK 24: Hanbury

A short circular walk from Hanbury Common. Easy walking mainly across grazing land but with some lane walking through the village. Exceptionally good views across the Dove valley.

Distance: 2 miles (4km)

Time: Allow 1 hour

Map: Pathfinder Sheet SK 02/12 Abbots Bromley.

How To Get There:

By Car – Access is by way of the A515 between Sudbury and Yoxall. Take the turning signed to Coton-in-the-Clay and soon after there is a turning right again for Hanbury. The picnic site is on your left before the village.

By Bus – There is a limited service from Uttoxeter and Burton.

Refreshments and Accommodation: There is a pub in the village and accommodation in nearby Tutbury.

Nearest Tourist Information: Burton-on-Trent. (01283) 516609.

Hanbury's existence has been very much determined by the constantly changing uses of the Forest of Needwood. Clearance of the woodland and enclosures of fields throughout the ages have led, however, to a landscape which is predominantly pastoral, but the woodlands of Marchington are a reminder of the extent of this ancient forest. As you approach the village, the church and water-tower stand out immediately. It is thought that, on the site of the church, there was once a nunnery established by King Ethelred in AD 680, but by all accounts it was destroyed by the marauding Danes 200 years later.

Victoria's Keeper of the Privy Purse

Hanbury seems to have retained its links with high society throughout

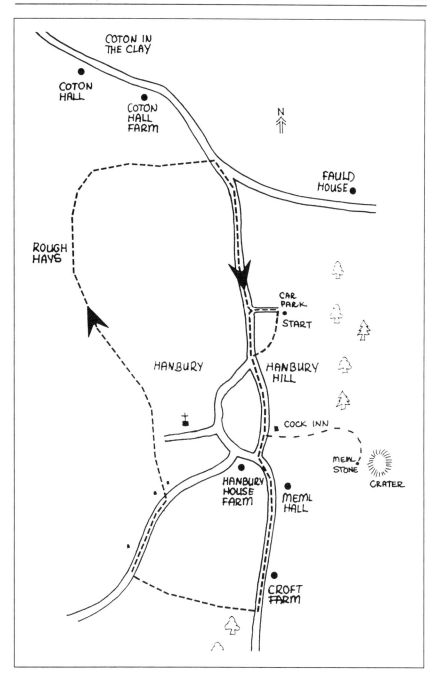

the centuries very much as a favoured location in Needwood Forest. Queen Victoria's Keeper of the Privy Purse, who also happened to be Axe Bearer of the Forest, was very fond of the area and indeed died nearby. In recognition of his affection, funds were made available for internal restoration work at the church, which is mainly medieval in origin. Queen Victoria also made a contribution to the building of the village school.

Start from Hanbury Common car-park and either make your way up through the common or return to the tarmac lane and turn left up to the village. Passing by the Cock Inn on your left, you'll see an interesting notice explaining a most unlikely tale. If it wasn't so tragic, you would think it was a spoof. At 11 minutes past 11 o'clock on November 27, 1944, there was an enormous explosion. Nearly 4000 tons of bombs stored 90 feet (30m) beneath the surface in old gypsum mines blew up. Unfortunately, 70 were killed and 18 people were never found. The damage in the surrounding villages and homesteads was extensive. The Cock Inn itself was so badly damaged that it had to be rebuilt. Strangely enough, Hanbury had received a similar shock in 1777 but not of the same magnitude and of a natural making. The parish register records that about 11 o'clock a 'smart shock' was received throughout the parish, the shock being a minor earth movement. Don't let this put you off your walk!

Just beyond the Cock Inn's children's playground area is a rough lane on the left. To visit the site of the explosion, an additional mile's walk, go along this lane and follow the red "Village Walk" waymarks to the memorial beside the crater. Retrace your steps from the memorial (please don't continue along the red route) to return to the Cock Inn's playground. Continue the few paces away from the Cock to the junction and turn left towards Burton, walking away from the village past the Memorial Hall and then Croft Farm.

About 150 yards beyond the farm is a stile on the right, opposite the red-brick built house "Sunny Breeze". Climb this and walk to the head of the long field. Ignore the stile on your right in the elbow-corner, instead look to the hedge across the top for a tricky stile, then once over walk ahead to the barred gate at the end of the pasture. Turn right along the road and follow it for about 300 yards, passing by a large nursing home. As the road bends right take the footpath on the left between the grounds of two houses, signposted as a footpath to Coton-in-the-Clay. Go through the fields, and, at the blue arrow, cross to the left of the hedge to reach the end of a rough lane, leading down from the church.

The Broad Dove

Continue ahead, if not visiting the church, to a barred gate. There are magnificent views from this vantage point of the broad Dove Valley and the Peak District beyond, to the left along the edge to Marchington Woods and to the right of Fauld Gypsum Works and Tutbury Castle.

Tutbury is a flourishing village with a number of attractions – the crystal glass works, the castle, historic church and sheepskin shop at the old corn mill. There is a locally produced leaflet informing the visitor about these attractions and there are a number of places to take refreshments.

Carry on to another gate, beyond which is a dead tree. Go ahead here, allowing an alternative path to fall away left beside a wooded cleft, once an old workings. Look ahead to the hilltop crowned with Scots Pines and thorn trees, known as Rough Hayes. Climb a stile and walk to the right of this. Head downslope towards the white-painted house, Coton Hall, to find the next stile nestling below a hollow oak tree. Go over it and bear left, so that you're still heading straight downhill with Coton Hall before you in the foreground. The path curves to the right to meet the field corner. At the gateway turn right and continue ahead along the dirt road to the next junction, where the stile is across the track. Cross it and walk ahead, moving closer to the right-hand corner as you proceed. Go over the stile and head for the white barred gate. Go through it and turn right, then right again up the tarmac lane to Hanbury Common car-park entrance.

WALK 25: Loggerheads and Burnt Wood

Easy walking along paths and woodland tracks.

Distance: 5 miles (9km)

Time: Allow 3 hours

Map: Pathfinder Sheet SJ 63/73 Market Drayton.

How To Get There:

By Car – Loggerheads is on the A53 between Newcastle-under-Lyme and Market Drayton. There is a limited amount of parking here.

By Bus – There is a regular service, Mondays to Saturdays, between Hanley and Market Drayton.

Refreshments and Accommodation: There are pubs at Loggerheads and Ashley. Limited accommodation.

Nearest Tourist Information: Newcastle-under-Lyme. (01782) 711964.

Loggerheads is small dormitory village mid-way between Newcastle-under-Lyme and Market Drayton. Nearby is Blore Heath, the site of a famous and bloody battle of the Wars of the Roses. Loggerheads, like Ashley, is a village that has grown up as the woodland of the area has been cleared.

Start at the main junction of roads at Loggerheads taking the B5026 road to Eccleshall. Climb for a while, then turn right opposite Pinewood Road and first left by the old Jubilee school dating from 1860. Immediately before the next chapel on the right there's a little path on the right signed to Goldenhill and Fair Oak. This leads up to a stile beneath an elderberry. Follow the left-hand field boundary up to a stile under a hollybush. Cross this, turn left and follow the field edge around to a stile.

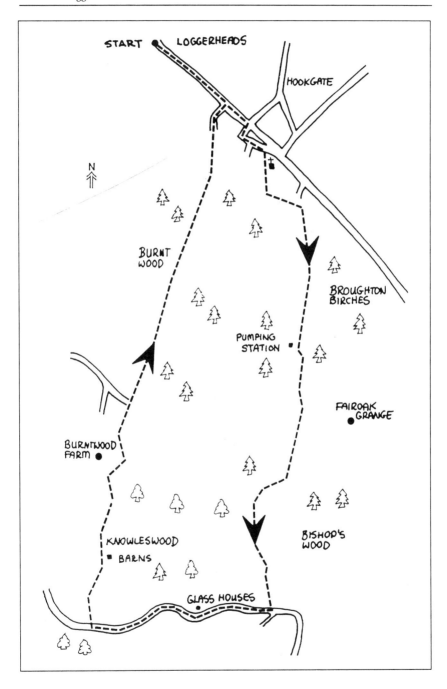

Forestry

Turn right and walk along the metalled road through arable land to a point where it bends left at the woodland edge near the pumping station. Go through the gate here and turn left. Rights of Way in these woods are few so be vigilant in following the correct paths. The path soon widens to a grassy road. Follow it around to the left past the field corner and in 75 metres go right at the fork. In a further 200 metres bear left at the junction of green roads as the main track curves away to the right. This steepening track is marked by numerous rounded stones at the surface. It eventually emerges onto a gravelled forest road at a corner. Turn right, walk for ten or so paces then go left down the obvious track. This soon becomes a sunken path to a gate and foot-bridge. Once over turn this turn left and walk down the long thin pasture above the stream, then the subsequent meadow to reach a metalled lane.

Turn right at the tarmac lane and pass by Glass Houses Farm, the track curving right by the farm buildings and up to a barred gate. Go through this and follow the concrete road crossing the field and rising. Follow this until you pass by a plantation of young trees on your right, with a more mature setting to your left ahead. You will see a set of double gates on the right.

The path is waymarked up the dry hollow to a gate at the top right of the field under hawthorns. Go through the gate and turn left. Walk up through the barred gate beyond the pylon and by the remains of Knowleswood Farm on the right, now being partly used as stables. Just beyond the buildings go ahead along the dirt track, skirting the edge of the woods to reach a stile beside a barred gate. Follow the just discernible track which winds through the field to a stile sited under oak and ash trees almost ahead of you. Burntwood Farm is on your left now and Smith's Rough to your right.

Burnt Wood

Keep company with the hedge on your left for 300 metres, then go through the gate and turn right, walking the short distance to a stile by the next gate beside a single pine tree. . Continue ahead, climbing steadily,. Eventually the track meets woodland again and leads back to a lane and the main B5026, where you turn left and retrace your steps.

WALK 26: Milwich

A short walk skirting Coton and returning by way of Milwich Church Easy walking in a little discovered area.

Distance: 2 miles (4km)

Time: Allow 1 hour

Map: Pathfinder Sheet SJ 83/93 Stone.

How To Get There:

By Car – Milwich is on the B5027 between Stone and Uttoxeter.

By Bus – Very infrequent weekly service.

Refreshments and Accommodation: There is a pub in the village and limited accommodation in the area. More is available at Stone. There is a limited amount of car-parking at the village hall but please consider local residents.

Nearest Tourist Information: Stafford. (01785) 40204.

Milwich is not renowned for its walking, but it should be, for the area offers a number of rewarding walks. Thanks to the interest of the parish council and the Conservation Volunteers, these paths are being re-opened for our use. The village itself nestles in a valley and is crossed by the Stone to Uttoxeter turnpike road dating from the late 18th century. One of the old toll houses (now a private residence) can still be seen opposite to the pub.

Milwich is huddled around the pleasant Green Man pub. The nearby church is unusual, in that it has a tower dating from the 15th century, but the rest was built in dark red brick, probably in the late 18th century. You'll also pass by the restored half-timbered hall. Across the road from the pub is the restored Community Centre, the starting point of our walk.

Turn right along Always Close, signposted for Garshall Green and

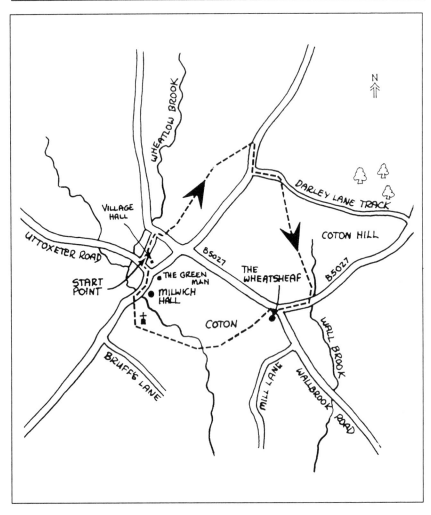

Mossgate. At the top end turn right at the T-junction and opposite the third pair of houses there is a stile set at the top of the bank on your left, 10 metres before the red brick barn. Climb this and walk alongside the hedge on your right. Go over the next two stiles in line and the path rises through the next field to a stile beside twin ash trees.

Go straight across the next pasture to a stile which leads to a minor road. Turn sharp right and follow this for 100 metres, then go left along the old green lane, falling gently with this ancient route to a stream in the shallow valley.

Secluded Valley

The valley is that of Wall Brook. Just before reaching the stream go right over a stile and trace the brook a few metres downstream, then cross it at the culvert and continue downstream, water to your right. The next stile is well hidden beneath hawthorns, so persevere! The brook is essentially ditched down the centre of this long pasture, simply remain with it to the little plank bridge. Cross this and continue down the shadowy valley, the brook now totally culverted beneath pastures on your left

Eventually, the stream re appears as a meandering course overhung by trees. Keep it to your left to reach the B5027 road. Turn right along this fairly busy road, in 250 metres coming to a sharp bend so it might be better to cross beforehand.

The Wheatsheaf

You reach a solid building on the left at the junction, the old Wheatsheaf public house which is currently closed (Summer 1996). So hold your thirst for a while longer and bear right with the B5027 towards Stone. In a matter of metres, just before the "No Footway" road sign, is a waymarked stile on your left. Climb this and skirt the rough enclosure on your right to a step stile. Once over this look ahead left to spot the stile in a gap in the tall hedge about 50 metres away. Go over this into a long, rough pasture.

Favour the right edge of this field and walk to its end, passing (but not crossing) a stile along the way. At the far right corner climb the stile, drop to and cross the footbridge over Gayton Brook and climb the stile just beyond it. The path curves to the right to reach a wire fence angling across the large field. Do not cross the stile here but remain outside the fence and walk up the slope towards the church on the rise ahead.

Enter the churchyard via the gate beneath the hollybush and walk past the church tower. In 10 metres go right at the fork in the graveyard path and leave the environs of the church by a stile in the corner. A further stile in the field corner to the right of the bungalow leads to a steep path down to the road. Bear right along this to find the Green Man pub in the centre of the village.

WALK 27: Onecote and the Hamps Valley

A circular walk in the quieter reaches of the upper Hamps valley. Easy walking mostly but can get very muddy in places.

Distance: Nearly 3 miles (5km)

Time: Allow: 1 hours

Map: Outdoor Leisure 24: The White Peak.

How To Get There:

By Car – Onecote is situated on the B5053 between Warslow and Bottom Houses (on A523). There is a limited amount of street parking in the hamlet.

By Bus – There is a very infrequent service from Leek

Refreshments and Accommodation: The local inn, the Jervis, serves food and there is accommodation available in the area.

Nearest Tourist Information: Leek. (01538) 381000

Start from the church. Georgian in origin and with a distinctive tower, this is a striking landmark in such a high moorland area. Walk to the main B5053, bear right, and proceed for a short distance to the first turning on the left. Follow this lane, which has a tarmac surface at first to beyond the farm. From here onwards, continue ahead on a very rough track, marshy in places but passable. Go past a ruined building, then through a number of gateways, always maintaining a path ahead. You come to a very marshy area and, at this point, there is a little footbridge over a stream. A farm appears before you and to the left of it you will see a stile. Cross it and proceed ahead down the lane to Ford, passing by a building with stone-mullioned windows.

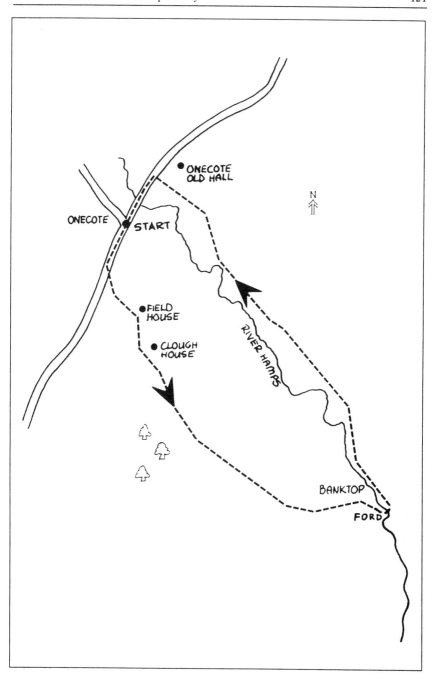

Ford

At the junction, by the telephone kiosk, go left and over the bridge. This is the infant River Hamps and your return journey will be along the lower slopes of the Hamps Valley between Ford and Onecote. This is the smallest of hamlets and still very much a farming community. Your way is to the left of the farmhouse, signposted, along an extremely muddy lane which winds its way to the right, by the barn, then through a wider section covered with agricultural implements.

Be warned, this can be really wet and muddy in inclement weather. Confronted with a number of possible routes take the open track, with barbed wire fencing, bearing slightly left towards the river. This track, with an aggregate surface, should be followed. You will see a stile adjacent to a barred gate. Cross this and the stream beyond and follow the track again, now with a pool to your left. Meet another track and bear right, still proceeding up the valley.

The track eventually bears right and up the hill towards Bullclough. You, however, continue ahead over the stile and then maintain a position above the flood plain with a fence on the right. There are dozens of meanders in this environ and would-be ox bow lakes forming in the valley bottom to your left, all good stuff of a geography lesson!.

There is a more difficult section ahead under the trees which requires sure footwork. Drop down to the stream, cross it and maintain a path towards Onecote, which is now coming into sight. Bear slightly right as you progress, rising gently and eventually climbing to the right of the trees sited on a small bluff. Here, you will find a stile in the drystone wall.

Cross it and maintain a path ahead, with a farm to your right and houses before you. The path falls to a stile in the hedge and then crosses a footbridge to the B5053. Turn left and, facing the traffic, pass by the Jervis Arms with its pleasant outdoor area next to the Hamps. The Staffordshire Moorlands is deservedly popular for walking and this corner is no exception.

WALK 28: The Ridwares

A short circular from Hamstall Ridware to Pipe Ridware.
Easy walking mainly across fields.

Distance: 3 miles (5km)

Time: Allow 1 hours

Map: Pathfinder Sheet SK 10/11 Rugeley and Lichfield North.

How To Get There:

By Car – Hamstall Rid ware is signposted from the B5014 between Uttoxeter and Handsacre or from the A515 at Yoxall.

By Bus – There is a very sparse weekly service.

Refreshments and Accommodation: There is a pub in the village and refreshments are also available for those visiting the Arts Centre. Limited accommodation is available in the Ridwares but there's more in Lichfield. There is a little street car-parking available but please park with consideration.

Nearest Tourist Information: Lichfield. (01543) 252109.

The Ridwares, the name belonging to a group of villages and hamlets located on the gently undulating slopes of the Trent Valley north west of Lichfield, means 'The River Folk'. Of all of the settlements Hamstall Rid ware is furthest away from the Trent. The village climbs gently from the pub to the church. The restored manor house, now the Rid ware Arts Centre, is open to the public on a regular basis.

The Ridwares

The Ridwares are a group of villages and hamlets which lie in this quiet part of the county. The church at Hamstall Ridware, lying in a beautiful setting across a field, is well worth a visit. There are other

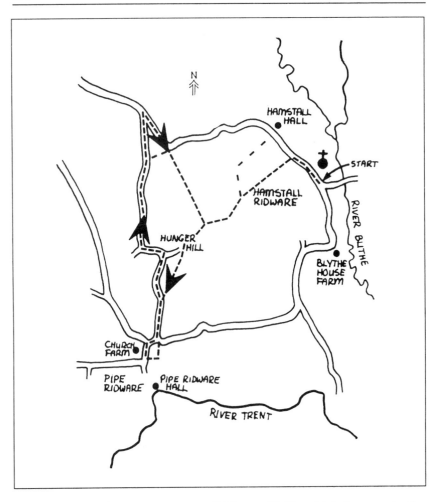

attractions in the area: Masevyn Ridware Hall, which is open to the public at certain times, and nearby Hanch Hall. Combined with an excursion to Lichfield, a visit to the Ridwares can be most enjoyable.

Start the walk from the gateway leading to the church of St Michael and the Angels. Turn right on the road and look for a stile on the left before houses. Cross it and follow the path up to the right-hand corner. Cross the stile and climb gently once again, keeping to the right-hand boundary to beyond the gate where you'll see a small pond. Turn right at the corner and follow the hedge towards a house at the top of the brow of Cowley Hill. Turn . Cross over the stile by the gate on the right.

Turn left on the track and walk ahead. Cross a stile into another field. Your way is to the left of the trig point, diagonally across the field, to a stile. There's a wonderful view ahead, despite Rugeley Power station.

Farming Country

Go through a pocket of woodland and two stiles. Then head downhill to cross another and to the right of the clump of hawthorns and to the right of a scar. Drop down to a stile in the hedge on the right. Walk ahead along the boundary but go left over a stile by the tree. . Proceed slightly right to the hedge on the right and follow this down to the lane in the far bottom corner.

Pipe Ridware

Cross the lane and go through the barred gate. There's an access on your right leading into the churchyard. Go through it. The church is now the Rid ware Theatre. At the lane, bear right and right again, then left to begin the return section. Follow this very quiet lane up the hill to a large farmhouse on the left known as Goldenhayfields. The lane begins to curve and on the right, beneath one of the oaks, is something of a stile. Cross it and head slightly right to the field corner to the right of the house. Cross over the boundary fence here and continue ahead to the gateway.

Bear right and, keeping the hedge to your left, proceed through a gateway to the next hedge boundary. Walk ahead until you return to the gateway at Hunger Hill (where you have been previously). Go over the stile on your left and retrace your steps to Hamstall Ridware. Alternatively, follow the track down a short distance until a stile appears on the right. Cross over this and walk down the field towards Hamstall Hall. The path comes out on to a tarmac lane, where it is possible to turn right, back towards the church.

WALK 29: Rushton Spencer

A circular walk around this North Staffordshire Village bordering Cheshire. Easy walking along tracks, through fields and along the reed fringed conduit supplying water to Rudyard Reservoir from the River Dane.

Distance: 4 miles (6.5km)

Time: Allow 2 hours

Map: Outdoor Leisure No 24: The White Peak.

How To Get There:

By Car – Rushton is on the main A523 between Leek and Macclesfield.

By Bus – Daily service between Manchester and Derby.

Refreshments and Accommodation: Rushton Spencer is extremely well blessed with public houses and there is accommodation available around the village. There is car-parking on the Staffordshire Way, route access being to the left of the Knot Inn and by the old station house.

Nearest Tourist Information: Leek. (01538) 381000

Start at the car-park on the Staffordshire Way as indicated above. Bear right out of the parking and picnic area and head along the disused railway towards Rudyard, but only for a short distance. This was once the North Staffordshire Railway linking Macclesfield to the Potteries and the Churnet Valley. On the other side of the first overbridge, there is an access stile at the top of the embankment on your left to a footpath above. Once on the bridge, turn left and go over the stile leading into the field beneath the church. Head for the churchyard, the path leads you up through it. Look out for the gravestone of Wilford Gibson, Rushton stationmaster 1946-1961.

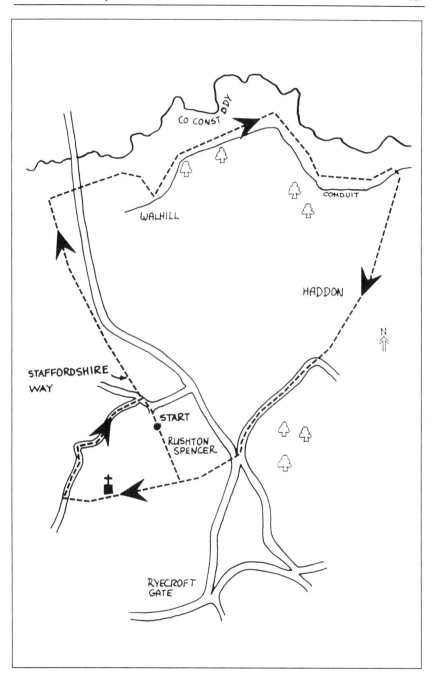

'Chappell in the Withernesse'

This isolated place of worship was referred to in earlier times as 'The Chappell in the Withernesse'. It is an unusual survival, for many churches of this period were replaced by larger stone structures. Rushton, however, remains small and inside it is still the wooden construction of medieval times. Continue along the track to a narrow road and bear right towards the village again. This pretty lane winds down Rushton Bank to a junction, where you bear right to the old station house. This superbly maintained dwelling dates from 1844, characteristically solid and built in mock Gothic-style. Cross the stile on your left and proceed along the Staffordshire Way in the direction of Macclesfield this time, a path which runs along the old trackbed where there is an aggregate surface.

Gritstone Trail

A path soon leads down the embankment to an information board. This is the meeting point of the Staffordshire Way and the Gritstone Trail, the latter extending through Cheshire to Lyme Park at Disley. Go right here under the railway track and make your way up to the A523. As this is potentially the most dangerous spot on the walk, walk carefully across the road to the stile on the other side, which leads to the green pastures of the River Dane floodplain. Follow the curve of the river terrace to another stile. After crossing this, bear right up to the feeder canal.

Feeding Rudyard Reservoir

Turn left once on the bank of the conduit and proceed along this delightful path. It is often lush with growth and rich in wildlife, something of a secretive place which can be very tranquil in summer. Follow the path to a stile and a bridge where the Gritstone Trail bears left. Your way is right, over the bridge and along a track which leads up the hill, with a valley to your left. Continue along it, passing two farms, until you reach a crossroads. Cross over and in a short distance you meet another lane.

Continue ahead to the main road by the pub, and turn right. Opposite there is a clearly defined path on the left before the old police station – the path goes alongside the conduit at first, but then bears right across the field to a footbridge, and the railway overbridge encountered earlier in the walk. The small church beyond is your landmark. Descend to the railway trackbed and go under the bridge, retracing your steps to the car-park.

WALK 30: Tyrley Wharf and Cheswardine

A walk between the hamlets of Tyrley Wharf and Cheswardine – which is actually in Shropshire! Easy walking through fields, returning along the towpath of the Shropshire Union Canal.

Distance: 6 miles (10km)

Time: Allow 3 hours

Map: Pathfinder Sheet SJ 63/73, number 829.

How To Get There:

By Car – Travel to Market Drayton, then on the A529 to Newport. At the Four Alls Inn turn left for Tyrley Locks.

By Bus – There is a very limited service from Market Drayton and Stafford.

Refreshments and Accommodation: There are pubs in Cheswardine.

Nearest Tourist Information: Market Drayton, Tel: (01630) 652139

One of the prettiest places to be on the Shropshire Union Canal has to be Tyrley Locks, just to the south of Market Drayton. Here cottages dating from the 1840s stand next to the busy locks through which boats pass during the long summer days. The countryside here is not well known although the paths are reasonable and since writing the first edition the author has investigated a number of paths in this western borderland between Staffordshire and Shropshire. More of the ramble is actually in Staffordshire but this is of no concern. This 6 mile ramble links Tyrley to the village of Cheswardine, with its fine church and Georgian houses.

Facing the cottages at Tyrley Locks turn left. The road dips as it bends right and left. Cross a stile ahead into a field. It seems so tranquil

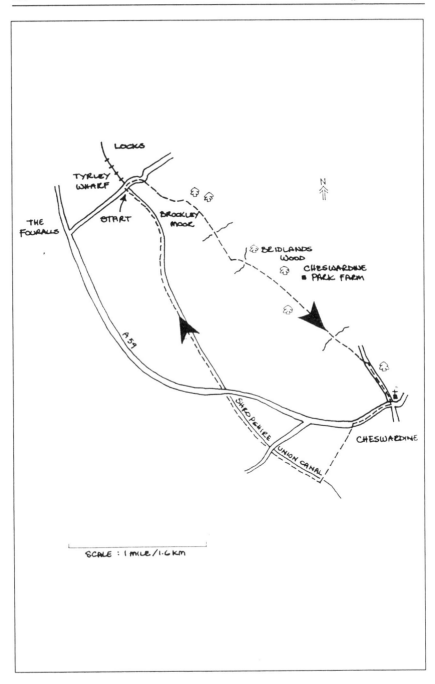

SCALE : 1 MILE / 1·6 KM

now, stepping into a different world which is so untouched. Keep right to follow the field's edge to reach a stile in a wall. Go over it and then proceed slightly left to the top field corner where you cross a track. Follow the line of trees ahead and on reaching a large oak head slightly left to the corner of a wood. Cross a footbridge here and make your way through a plantation.

Walk ahead through a field to another pocket of wood but proceed for approximately 100 metres only before turning right to cross a footbridge and by a pool. Go over a stile to enter a large field. Keep ahead here and you will see Cheswardine Park farm to your left. Pass by a pool and at the top corner of the field go through a gap, and continue ahead with a hedge to your left. Cross a stile into another small wood where there are several paths. You, however, keep left and head between two pools to exit at a stile on the right.

Go ahead, now keeping company with a hedge on your left. The path reaches a woodland. There's a stile which is entirely overgrown so follow the line of path just to the left of it and then by a stream . Cross a stile and head slightly left up the large field towards another wood. You join a bridleway at the boundary. Keep right and cross a stile. Follow the bridleway to the village of Cheswardine. You cannot fail to miss the church. This is the home of a famous gingerbread maker and the version made hereabouts is said to be an aphrodisiac.

In Cheswardine go right at the road (left if you require refreshment). Leave the village along a road to soon reach a group of houses. Go left over a stile just before. Walk down the field to pass a pool and cross a stile. Keep ahead to cross a second stile at the next boundary. Go ahead again to another stile. You will see a canal bridge to your left. Turn left through a gateway to it. Once over the bridge cut right to join the towpath for a two mile return to Tyrley. You will find that the cuttings are exceptionally beautiful.

Also of interest:

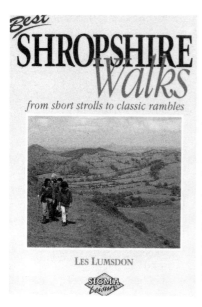

BEST SHROPSHIRE WALKS:
short strolls to classic rambles

This best selling and revised book by Les Lumsdon introduces 30 walks in an area which has rightly become popular with walkers. The book has been thoroughly updated to meet the demands of those who seek the tranquillity of Shropshire, escaping to delightful villages such as Claverley, Neen Sollars and Myddle. This revised edition of Shropshire Walks is not only strengthened by new and enhanced walks, but also contains up-to-the-minute information on pubs, refreshment, local attractions and public transport.   £6.95

BEST PUB WALKS IN THE BLACK COUNTRY

Chris Rushton

£6.95

PUB WALKS IN NORTH STAFFORDSHIRE

Les Lumsdon and Chris Rushton

£6.95

BEST PUB WALKS IN HEREFORDSHIRE

Les Lumsdon

£6.95

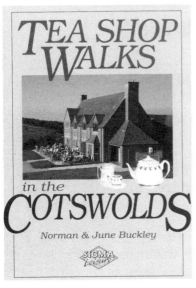

The Cotswolds:

TEA SHOP WALKS IN THE COTSWOLDS

Norman & June Buckley have written the perfect book for those who love to combine a walk in the English countryside with afternoon tea – that most English of pastimes. No other area in Britain has as many tea shops as the Cotswolds. This new book of 26 walks takes the reader the length and breadth of the area, visiting both the popular towns and tiny villages. The walks average 5-6 miles and each features a tea shop that welcomes walkers. *£6.95*

WALKING ON & AROUND THE COTSWOLD WAY

Walking a long distance footpath is an attractive prospect but not always a practical one. David Hunter shows that walking the route in short sections is a preferable alternative allowing the walker to pick the time, the place and the pace to suit his own requirements. The routes are fully detailed, but space and time has been left for leisurely exploration of places of interest which are well described in the text. Clear maps, many photographs and a useful information section all combine to assist the explorer on his way. *£6.95*

PUB WALKS IN THE COTSWOLDS

Laurence Main has written the most comprehensive guide to the best pubs and most interesting walks in the area. Ghostly tales add to the fascination. *£6.95*

A further selection:

WALKING IN HAUNTED GLOUCESTERSHIRE

Florence Jackson & Gordon Ottewell hold your hand while walking in ghostly footsteps. Don't venture out alone! £6.95

RAMBLES IN NORTH NOTTINGHAMSHIRE

Malcolm McKenzie explores this unfrequented area. £6.95

NEWARK AND SHERWOOD RAMBLES

Also by Malcolm McKenzie, who shows that there's more to the area than Robin Hood! £6.95

EAST CHESHIRE WALKS: from Peak to Plain

This book, by Graham Beech, first appeared in 1985 and was the first book of walks published by Sigma. Thousands of copies later, in 1996, it is now in its THIRD EDITION! Over 200 miles of walks ranging from a three-mile easy saunter to a 20-mile challenge walk over the highest hills! £6.95

WEST CHESHIRE WALKS

The perfect companion to our East Cheshire guidebook. Gentle walks by Jen Darling. £5.95

CHESHIRE WALKS WITH CHILDREN

Nick Lambert's book will occupy the whole family. Walks to enjoy, quizzes to answer, things to look for – children will be asking to go on another walk, not finding excuses to stay indoors! £7.95

PUB WALKS IN CHESHIRE

A well-established book by Jen Darling covering country walks throughout the county with tried and tested pubs to welcome ramblers. £6.95

BEST PUB WALKS IN & AROUND CHESTER & THE DEE VALLEY

John Haywood explores the historic area based on Chester and Wrexham. Bags of history, superb pubs . £6.95

All of our books are available from your local bookshop. In case of difficulty, or to obtain our complete catalogue, please contact:

Sigma Leisure, 1 South Oak Lane, Wilmslow, Cheshire SK9 6AR
Phone: 01625 – 531035
Fax: 01625 – 536800
E-mail: sigma.press@zetnet.co.uk

ACCESS and VISA orders welcome – call our friendly sales staff or use our 24 hour Answerphone service! Most orders are despatched on the day we receive your order – you could be enjoying our books in just a couple of days. Please add £2 p&p to all orders.